CITY LIGHTS

City Lights

Essays on financial institutions
and markets
in the City of London

E. VICTOR MORGAN
Professor of Economics,
University of Reading

R. A. BREALEY
Barclaytrust Professor of Investment, and
Director of the Institute of Finance and Accounting,
London Graduate School of Business Studies

B. S. YAMEY
Professor of Economics,
University of London (London School of Economics)

PAUL BAREAU
Economic Adviser,
International Publishing Corporation

Published by
THE INSTITUTE OF ECONOMIC AFFAIRS
1979

First published in April 1979 by
THE INSTITUTE OF ECONOMIC AFFAIRS
© The Institute of Economic Affairs 1979

ISSN 0305-814X
ISBN 0-255 36119-X

Printed in England by
Goron Pro-Print Co. Ltd., Lancing, Sussex
Set in Monotype Times Roman 11 on 12 point

Contents

City Lights

Preface

The *IEA Readings* have been devised to refine the market in economic thinking by presenting varying approaches to a single theme in one volume. They are intended primarily for teachers and students of economics but are edited to help non-economists in industry and government who want to know how economics can explain the activities with which they are concerned.

Readings 19 comprises essays by economists on four main aspects of British financial institutions. It has been compiled to show what light economics can throw on the working of the institutions that assemble personal saving, the capital market which translates saving into investment and enables uncertainty to be minimised, the markets that bring together buyers and sellers of basic commodities, and the relatively recent development of Euro-currencies.

Most of these market institutions are part of 'the City' of London, which engages in the most important financial transactions in the world and earns large sums of foreign currencies for Britain by supplying private services for overseas customers. The City has been the subject of recurrent criticism in the post-war years, most recently on the ground that it has retarded the growth of investment, earlier that its overseas earnings were of little consequence.

There has also been much criticism of the City as being beyond political control, comprising family businesses with public school, upper-class connections, and operating in the manner of members of a club rather than of competitors in the market. Such attitudes have coloured opinion on the City, and in several studies since the IEA was founded in 1957 it has tried instead to analyse the economic working of City institutions in order to sort the wheat of analysis from the chaff of prejudice. In 1958 Mr William M. Clarke[1] showed that its contribution to the balance of payments by its overseas earnings was much more considerable than had been claimed by critics such as Mr (now Sir) Andrew Shonfield, Professor A. C. L. Day and others. Also in 1958 Mr Paul Bareau wrote a study of sterling and the sterling system and showed that it was of much more advantage to Britain that its critics had argued.[2] In 1965 Mr Clarke

---

[1] *The City's Invisible Earnings.*

[2] *The Future of the Sterling System.*

wrote a longer study of the City as the world's banker, as a dealer in foreign exchange and gold, its insurance market which underwrote risks all over the world, its commodity markets, its world-wide shipping services, and its capital market institutions.[3]

The contribution made by the City to the economy must be related to the degree to which it is competitive in supplying services and to its freedom from the resistance to change with which British trade unions have become associated. Some restrictive practices remain, although on a comparatively minor scale; in a world market for banking, insurance, merchanting and shipping, the City has to operate by keeping its efficiency high and its costs relatively low.

The four essays now assembled in this *Readings* are especially timely when the report of the Wilson Committee, appointed on 5 January 1977, is expected some time in 1979. Many of its inquiries are anticipated in these essays:

'. . . the role and function, at home and abroad, of financial institutions in the United Kingdom and their value to the economy; . . . the provision of funds for industry and trade, . . . the expansion of these institutions, including the . . . public sector.'

Whatever the political motivation for establishing the Committee and whatever the political prejudices incorporated in some of the evidence it has received, it is still desirable for students and teachers of economics, for citizens generally, and not least for people who work in the City, to understand what its financial institutions are doing, why they are doing it, and the consequences that emerge. In the work of analysis economics is indispensable in understanding the functions and problems of the City and the consequences of subjecting it to increasing government control.

March 1979   ARTHUR SELDON

---

[3] *The City in the World Economy.*

1. Personal Saving and Financial Institutions

E. VICTOR MORGAN
Professor of Economics,
University of Reading

The Author

E. VICTOR MORGAN was born in 1915 and educated at Warwick School and Sidney Sussex College, Cambridge. Professor of Economics at the University of Reading since 1974; previously held chairs in economics at the University College of Swansea (1945-66) and the University of Manchester (1966-74). Visiting Professor at Columbia University, New York (1953 and 1957), and at Simon Fraser University, British Columbia (1967). Chairman of the Economists' Advisory Group, and a member of the IEA's Advisory Council.

Professor Morgan's publications include *Studies of British Financial Policy 1914-25* (Macmillan, 1951); *The Structure of Property Ownership in Great Britain* (OUP, 1960); (with W. A. Thomas) *The Stock Exchange* (Elek Books, 1964, 2nd Edn. 1969); *A History of Money* (Penguin Books, 1965); (with Ann D. Morgan) *The Economics of Public Policy* (Edinburgh University Press, 1972).

For the IEA he has written *Monetary Policy for Stable Growth* (Hobart Paper 27, 1964, 3rd Edn. 1969), (with Ann D. Morgan) *Gold or Paper?* (Hobart Paper 69, 1976), and contributions to *Not Unanimous* (1960), *Agenda for a Free Society* (1961), and *Crisis '75...?* (Occasional Paper Special (No. 43), 1975).

1. SAVING AND INVESTMENT

Saving in modern industrial societies is provided by households (personal saving), by the retained profits of companies in the private sector, and by the surpluses, if any, of public corporations, the central government and local authorities.

Household or personal saving plays a vital role in a market economy for several reasons. It is the way in which ordinary people can acquire assets and build up a 'stake in the country'; it is the only pool of mobile resources that can be switched quickly to finance any type of investment anywhere; and it is the 'raw material' of financial institutions. The retained profits of companies and public corporations are very largely used to finance their own investment. And when the government has a budget surplus, the proceeds are lent directly to other parts of the government or public sector. Company and 'public' saving thus largely by-pass the financial system.

Only a small part of household saving is used directly to finance investment[1] by savers; some of the rest is lent directly, e.g. by the purchase of company shares or national savings; but most of it is placed with financial institutions, e.g. deposited with banks or building societies or paid in life assurance premiums and contributions to pension funds. These institutions then re-lend the money to other households, to companies, to the public sector and (subject to exchange control restrictions) overseas. The essential role of financial institutions is, therefore, to mobilise household savings and distribute them to investors whoever and wherever they may be.

Strong upward trend in personal saving

In the early post-war years, household saving fell very low, largely because people were re-building stocks of consumer durables run down during the war. At the same time, companies were encouraged or compelled to plough back profits by restrictions on dividends, and it was fashionable for government to run a budget surplus as a remedy against inflation. During the past 20 years there has been a strong upward trend in household saving as a proportion of total

---

[1] Unless otherwise stated, 'investment' here means the accumulation of real assets (fixed capital and stocks), not the acquisition of securities.

saving, though the rise has been much faster at some times than at others.

Table 1 shows saving, investment and net lending by each of the main sectors in three recent years, 1971, 1974 and 1977. Household saving grew over the five years from 24 to 44 per cent of the total. Investment by the household sector fell from 19 to 16 per cent, and its net lending rose from £784 million to £8,699 million.

Even these figures do not do full justice to the importance of household saving, since they are calculated before taking account of depreciation and stock appreciation. These items are much more important for companies and public corporations than for the other sectors. Net saving (after deducting depreciation and stock appreciation from the gross figure) in 1977 was as follows:

	£ *million*
Households	9,664
Companies	1,540
Central government	−1,935
Other public sector	− 300
Total	8,969

Two other features should be noted. First, the years from 1974 to 1977 were unusual both because of the very large government deficit and because of the high values for stock appreciation resulting from rapid inflation. Both these influences reduced total net saving and raised the proportion of household saving to the total. Secondly, both total saving and household saving are lower in the UK than in other EEC countries and much lower than in Japan, though about the same as in the USA. Figures for the UK and the main EEC countries are shown in Table 2 (page 6).

UK's low rate of saving and investment

The average for 1971-3 shows the relationships that were typical of the late 1960s and early 1970s before the recession following the 1973-74 oil crisis. During the recession, the public sector in most countries ran into deficit and this is reflected in the reduced total saving of 1975, the latest year for which comparable figures are available. There was a marked rise in household saving in the UK, but it was still lower than in any of the other countries and barely

TABLE 1
SAVING[1] AND INVESTMENT[2]
BY MAIN SECTORS, 1971, 1974 and 1977

			£ million
Personal (household)	1971	1974	1977
Saving	2,956	8,187	13,863
Investment	2,172	2,974	5,164
Net lending	784	5,213	8,699
Companies[3]			
Saving	5,342	8,879	13,256
Investment	4,915	13,657	16,942
Net lending	427	–4,778	–3,686
Central Government			
Saving	2,485	451	–1,494
Investment	653	973	1,410
Net lending	1,832	– 522	–2,904
Other 'Public'[4]			
Saving	1,722	2,293	5,615
Investment	3,975	6,628	8,518
Net lending	–2,253	–4,335	–2,903
Total			
Saving	12,505	19,810	31,240
Investment	11,715	24,232	32,034
Net lending[5]	790	–4,422	– 794

Source: National Income and Expenditure, 1967-77, HMSO, 1978, Table 13.1.

Notes
1. Saving is before providing for depreciation and stock appreciation and includes capital transfers.
2. Investment is gross fixed capital formation plus increase in value of stocks and work in progress.
3. Total of industrial and commercial and financial companies.
4. Local authorities and public corporations.
5. Total net lending equals surplus on current balance of payments (lending to foreigners), allowing for statistical errors.

TABLE 2
NET SAVING AS PERCENTAGE OF GROSS DOMESTIC PRODUCT

	Total		Household	
	1971-3 average	*1975*	*1971-3 average*	*1975*
Belgium	16·2	12·8	13·3	13·0
France	15·0	10·8	8·8	13·3
Germany	15·9	9·5	8·6	9·4
Italy	13·5	9·7	15·4	n.a.
Netherlands	18·6	12·9	10·3	9·8
UK	*9·9*	*4·9*	*4·0*	*6·8*

Note: There are some differences in the definition of the household sector and in the treatment of capital consumption between countries and these may somewhat exaggerate the difference between the UK and other countries.

half that of France and Belgium. A low rate of saving has its counterpart in a low rate of investment,[2] and it was concern over the low rate of investment in the UK that was one of the main reasons for setting up the (Wilson) Committee to Review the Functioning of Financial Institutions.

Saving, and especially household saving, is the raw material of the financial system, and however efficient financial institutions may be, they cannot distribute to investors more money than they receive in savings. So, if the Wilson Committee was concerned about the low level of investment, the first question they asked might well have been:

'Why has the UK had so little net saving?'

In the event the Committee does not seem to have asked this question, but instead has posed a very different one:

'How can financial institutions cope with the flow of savings they are likely to receive?'

This paper will consider both these questions, and will argue that the problems implied in the second are illusory, but that the first is likely to remain a cause for real concern.

---

[2] In the years 1974 to 1976 domestic investment exceeded saving by the substantial amount of the balance-of-payments deficit.

2. WHY SO LITTLE SAVING?

The low rate of total saving, in relation to gross domestic product (GDP) in Britain, is due partly to a low level of household saving and partly to the offsetting in recent years of a large part of the private saving by deficits (*negative* saving) in the public sector. Public and private saving tend to be inversely related to each other; given the rate of state spending, a public sector deficit means that government is taking less in taxes (and therefore leaving the private sector more income out of which to save) than if the deficit had been smaller. Hence, the rise in household saving shown by the figures in Table 1 may have been in part a consequence of the rising public sector deficit.

The real problem, however, is why over many years household saving has been lower in Britain than in other major countries of the EEC. The explanation is even more elusive because two important forms of saving—through life assurance and pension funds—are much more highly developed in the UK than on the Continent. Life assurance premiums per head of the population are a third higher in Britain than in Germany, three times as high as in France, nine times as high as in Italy. Comprehensive figures for pension funds are not available, but it is well-known that the practice of funding occupational pension schemes (accumulating contributions during working life in a fund from which pensions are drawn) is more widespread in Britain than in the rest of Europe.

Lower incomes, higher consumption?

Many possible explanations have been suggested. In terms of *real* income per head (i.e. allowing for inflation) Britain is now substantially worse off than France, Germany, Belgium and the Netherlands. This difference is only recent, however; the low UK savings ratio was just as apparent when incomes were much more equal than they are now. Moreover, Ireland and Italy still have lower per capita incomes than the UK but substantially higher savings ratios.

A more plausible explanation is the slow UK growth rate. Some widely accepted theories of consumer expenditure[3] suggest that spending habits are adjusted only gradually to changes in income; if so, it is reasonable to expect that the rapid growth of income in the

---

[3] e.g. Milton Friedman, *A Theory of the Consumption Function,* Princeton University Press, Princeton, N.J., 1957.

EEC (and even more so in Japan) would be accompanied by high savings ratios.

The economic and social structure of a community may have implications for its propensity to save. Fairly obvious differences between the UK and other European countries are the relatively low share both of agriculture and of small business in the UK. Both farmers and small businessmen are traditionally regarded as thrifty, partly because they find borrowing difficult and so have to rely on their savings to expand their operations.

Higher government spending?

The volume of (government and other) public expenditure offers another possible explanation. Here it is necessary to distinguish between public spending on consumption and transfer payments, such as social security benefits, that go back into household incomes. Public consumption, by central and local authorities combined, is slightly higher in the UK than in Germany, and a lot higher than in other EEC countries, the USA and Japan. Figures for 1975 are as shown in Table 3.

TABLE 3
GOVERNMENT CONSUMPTION AS PERCENTAGE
OF GDP, 1975

	%		%
France	14·4	Italy	13·6
Germany	21·1	USA	19·3
Belgium	17·1	Japan	11·1
Netherlands	18·0	*UK*	*22·2*

Higher tax rates?

The amount of private saving that will take place with any given volume of public expenditure may also be influenced by the tax system. The UK relies more heavily on direct taxes and less on commodity taxes than do European countries; it has higher marginal tax rates on large incomes; and it discriminates against saving by describing income from property accumulated through saving as 'unearned' and taxing it at even higher rates than so-called 'earned' income.

The volume of saving may be influenced by the facilities provided by financial institutions and by incentives through tax relief and subsidies offered by governments. Life assurance and funded pension schemes are much more highly developed in the UK than in most other countries. Other institutions—banks, building societies and savings banks—offer much the same range of deposit facilities here and in Europe. Savings deposits in banks are less widely used here, but this is balanced by the larger role of building societies. The one feature of Continental banking that does not have a close parallel here is the small local savings bank that both collects savings and makes loans over a limited area and so becomes closely identified with its own community. The existence of such institutions may offer some encouragement to saving but it is difficult to believe that it is very important.

Incentives to saving?

All European governments encourage saving of one kind or another. The common methods include running savings banks through the Post Office at less than full economic costs; exempting income on small savings from tax; tax concessions for life assurance and pension contributions; and bonus payments on contractual savings schemes, often related to house purchase. It is very difficult to compare the net effects of many diverse schemes, but a recent review concluded that (apart from the treatment of 'unearned income') British schemes were no less generous than those of other EEC countries.[4]

Neither the UK nor other countries have gone far towards solving the problem of protecting savers against the erosion of the real value of their savings by inflation; and the UK has suffered more in this way than most other Western countries. It would seem that the prospect of losing value through inflation would be a strong deterrent to saving, but the evidence is not wholly consistent. Ireland and Italy have relatively *high* inflation rates combined with *high* household savings ratios, and the UK ratio rose during the early 1970s when inflation was accelerating. This led the Bank of England to advance the hypothesis that people *increase* their saving at times of rapid inflation in order to maintain the real value of their bank balances and other liquid assets.[5] An effect in the opposite direction is likely to be the pressure of inflation on people living on fixed incomes to induce some of them to sell securities and 'live on capital'.

---

[4] E. Victor Morgan and Richard Harrington, *Capital Markets in the EEC*, Wilton House, 1976, pp. 342-6.

[5] Bank of England *Quarterly Bulletin*, March 1976, pp. 53-72.

A committee of the OECD which studied the capital markets of member countries in the 1960s produced an interesting piece of relevant evidence. They distinguished between what they called 'national account saving' (*net* saving as we have used it here) and 'financial saving' (*gross* acquisition of financial assets). It is not possible to derive a complete picture of 'financial saving' from the available information but a minimum estimate can be gained by adding to the net acquisitions of Table 1 the value of known personal borrowings. For 1977, these were as follows:

		£ *million*
Bank loans, other than for house purchase		1,050
Trade credit from retailers and public corporations		– 363
Loans for house purchase:		
Building societies	4,096	
Other	152	
		4,248
Sale of company and overseas securities		1,912
Total		6,847

The net acquisition of financial assets (i.e. net lending) by households in 1977 was £8,699 million, so we can conclude that gross acquisitions were at least £15,546 million, of which at least £6,847 million (44 per cent) went to other units in the household sector.

The OECD committee compared 'financial saving' and 'national account saving' for Germany, the USA, France, Japan and the UK, with the results shown in Table 4.

TABLE 4
SAVING AS A PERCENTAGE OF PERSONAL DISPOSABLE INCOME, 1960-65*

	Financial %	National Account %
Germany	9·5	13·5
USA	8·7	5·7
France	9·0	8·2
Japan	21·6	17·2
UK	*8·3*	*5·0*

*OECD, *Capital Markets Study,* Paris, 1967, Vol. II, p. 16.

Japan stands out as having much higher savings by both measures but, as between the other four countries, financial savings are very similar whereas national account saving is much lower in the UK and the US. Putting the point another way, the proportion of gross financial savings by households that is offset by the borrowing of other households (39 per cent in the UK, 34 per cent in the US) is much higher than in the other countries.

Causes of high UK household borrowing

This high household borrowing may be due to three causes: new borrowing to finance consumption (e.g. by hire purchase); new borrowing to finance investment (e.g. bank or building society loans); and sales of securities to finance either investment or consumption. Consumer credit is probably more highly developed in the UK than on the Continent, but less so than in the US. Borrowing to finance household investment is mainly for house purchase, again probably rather easier in the UK than on the Continent. Household sales of company and overseas securities (£1,912 million) have been large for many years; they could be used to finance investment or could simply represent switching into other assets, but it seems likely that a substantial part is to finance consumption by households suffering the combined pressures of high taxes and inflation.

Thus the reasons for the low rate of household saving in the UK are very complex. It is possible to suggest many explanations, some more plausible than others, but with the information at present available it is impossible to test any of them rigorously. The explanations that look the most promising (not necessarily in order of importance) are:

- the slow growth of output and real income,
- the low share of agriculture and small business in the economy,
- the high level of government and other 'public' consumption,
- the tax system,
- the pressure exerted by taxation and inflation towards 'living on capital', and
- the relative ease of borrowing to finance both home ownership and consumption.

3. HOW MUCH SAVING DO WE WANT?

Saving is required to provide resources for investment, including any overseas lending that may arise from a surplus in the balance of payments. Hence, in order to ask how much saving we want we must also ask how much investment we require for the 'regeneration of British industry' and for the balance-of-payments surplus that may arise (unless dissipated by short-sighted domestic policies) from North Sea oil.

The poor performance of the UK economy is due to many causes of which the low rate of investment is only one. 'Regeneration' will require much more than increased investment. Nevertheless, the UK has been a low-saving, low-investing economy for a long time, and higher investment is one of the necessary conditions for a higher growth rate. The low rate of industrial investment is not related to high investment in other sectors, as sometimes suggested, but to a low *total*. UK investment is lower than that of other EEC countries not only in industry, but commerce, transport and even housing, and the distribution between major categories is very similar in the UK and other EEC countries. A rise in industrial investment is, therefore, likely to require a roughly similar rise in total domestic investment. Moreover, if the development of North Sea oil is not to result in a big loss of other export markets or much increased competition from non-oil imports, we shall have to meet a good deal of our reduced oil bill by overseas lending (including the repayment of debt).

Potential UK investment: implications of differing assumptions

Table 5 gives a few figures to show the potential amount of investment, and therefore saving, that may be required. They are not forecasts but merely show the *implications* of certain simple assumptions. Their purpose is to put into perspective figures for the growth of savings that have been bandied about in recent discussions.

Gross domestic investment (excluding stock appreciation) in the UK during 1976 was £23·8 billion, financed by domestic saving after providing for stock appreciation of £22·4 billion and a current account balance-of-payments deficit of £1·4 billion.

The first assumption of Table 5 is that growth in real terms will average 3 per cent between 1976 and 1985 and that there will be no change in the 1976 ratio (19·5 per cent) of gross investment to GDP. Domestic investment would then be about £31 billion (at 1976 prices) in 1985. The second and third assumptions allow for an increase in the ratio of gross investment to GDP to 25 per cent (about that attained by France and Germany during most of the 1960s and early 1970s) and for a balance-of-payments surplus of £2 billion a year, which would give a total of domestic and overseas investment, at 1976 prices, of £42 billion.

Many of the figures discussed in relation to financial institutions assume the continuation of high inflation rates. Our fourth set of assumptions therefore adds an inflation rate averaging 10 per cent a year, and our fifth includes an allowance for stock appreciation; this would imply investment and saving of around £100 billion, at current prices, by 1985.

TABLE 5
POTENTIAL UK INVESTMENT IN 1985

£ *billion*

Assumption 1
Growth at 3% p.a. 1976-85
Gross Investment at 1976 proportion of GDP at
market price (19·5%)   31

Assumption 2
As assumption 1, but gross investment 25% of GDP   40

Assumption 3
As assumption 2 but with £2 billion
balance-of-payments surplus   42

Assumption 4
As assumption 3 but with 10 per cent inflation rate   94

Assumption 5
As assumption 4 but allowing for stock appreciation   100

Growth of personal saving in the 1980s uncertain but crucial

The proportion of total saving that will be made by households is very uncertain, in view of the violent swings already noted for the recent past. On the average of the five years to 1977, household savings accounted for just under half the total excluding stock appreciation. The maintenance of such a proportion would imply a marked recovery, compared to 1976, both in public and company saving. Even so, it suggests that household saving of the order of £20 billion at 1976 prices and nearly £50 billion if inflation averages 10 per cent a year would be required in 1985 if the quite modest assumptions of the preceding paragraphs are to be realised.

These are the figures we should have in mind when asking:

'Can the financial institutions cope?'

These projections would imply a proportion of personal saving (before allowing for depreciation and stock appreciation) to GDP of about 12½ per cent compared with 10·2 per cent in 1976 and only 5·2 per cent in 1971. Both company saving and 'public' saving have serious disadvantages. Company saving impairs the freedom of shareholders to do what they wish with their earnings, and is likely to distort the allocation of resources. 'Public' saving when combined with high public expenditure implies tax rates that have strong disincentive effects. If we are to avoid these evils and still get the saving necessary to finance the investment we want, a continued upward trend in personal saving is essential.

4. CAN THE FINANCIAL INSTITUTIONS COPE?

Personal savers have shown by their behaviour that they want either liquidity, which they can get from deposits with banks, savings banks or building societies, or long-term security of income, which they can get by contractual saving through life assurance and pension schemes or, to a lesser extent, through the purchase of government securities. Increases in personal holdings of these assets in 1977 were:

	£ *million*
Notes, coin and bank deposits	1,049
Building society deposits	5,979
National savings	1,190
Other public sector securities	701
Life assurance and pension funds	6,121
	15,040

The total of these five items amounted to over 96 per cent of the total of 'financial savings' (page 10).

(i) *Wilson Committee and the insurance and pensions industry*

These flows have interesting implications for the long-term future of banks and building societies, but the main question raised by the Wilson Committee is whether the insurance companies and pension funds can cope with the likely inflow of funds to them and, in particular, whether they can provide industry with the funds it will want within the framework of the existing equity market.

Over the decade 1966 to 1976 the annual addition to the funds of insurance companies and pension schemes was growing at an average of 16½ per cent. If this rate continued to 1985 it would give an annual inflow in that year of £26 billion. The past increase has been mainly due to inflation; but the inflow at 1976 prices is likely to be about £8 billion by the mid-1980s, and an average inflation rate of 10 per cent would raise it to nearly £20 billion.

These figures can be cut down to size by comparing them with those given in Tables 1 and 2, and in earlier parts of the text. In 1976 the increase in life and pension funds amounted to 24 per cent of gross investment (excluding stock appreciation) in the economy as a whole; to 38 per cent of 'financial saving' and to 70 per cent of the net acquisition of financial assets by the personal sector. An inflow of £8 billion to insurance companies and pension funds in 1985 would be under 20 per cent of the gross investment implied in assumption 3 to Table 5. An inflow of £20 billion would be only 21 per cent of the investment implied in assumption 4. If household saving formed half of total saving and gross and net acquisition of financial assets bore the same proportion to household saving as in 1976, gross acquisitions would amount to £57 billion and net acquisitions to £30 billion. An inflow of £20 billion would thus be about 67 per cent of net acquisitions and about 35 per cent of gross acquisitions. All these percentages are lower than the corresponding ones for 1976.

There is thus nothing alarming about the overall picture when the prospective flows are set in their proper context.

(ii) *The equity markets and the role of the institutions*

The position in the equity markets is rather more complex. It is well known that, for many years past, institutional purchases of ordinary shares have exceeded the amount of new issues. This is the inevitable counterpart of the net sales by the personal sector (Section 2). Surveys of share ownership have shown that, as one would expect, personal holdings are concentrated in people over middle age and with fairly substantial assets. It was suggested earlier that personal sales can be largely explained by the combined pressures of taxation and inflation on such people. Had the institutions not been net buyers, these pressures would have pushed down equity prices and made industrial investment even less attractive.

These trends necessarily imply a rise in the proportion of ordinary shares in the hands of institutions. A recent survey by the Department of Trade has shown that the proportion (by market value) in the beneficial ownership of persons fell from 54 per cent in 1963 to 37·5 per cent in 1975. Over the same period, the holdings of insurance companies and pension funds rose from 16·4 to 32·7 per cent.

By projecting these trends, some on the Left[6] have conjured up the bogey-man of a group of financial institutions dominating the equity market. This collective personality is accused of all sorts of misbehaviour with scant regard for plausibility or even consistency. He wields irresponsible power, but he does nothing to induce incompetent industrial managements to mend their ways; he is ruled by the desire for gain but he will not provide adequate finance for profitable enterprises; he buys shares when prices are high and sells —or at least refrains from buying—when they are low, thus causing markets to become increasingly volatile.

A slightly different version of this grim fairy tale is the forecast, put about by some stockbrokers, of an equity famine forcing share prices up to inordinate heights, and presumably making it very cheap and easy to raise funds for investment.

Realities and fairy tales

It is impossible to forecast in detail the flow of funds between different sections of the capital market, but we can consider some of the realities which will determine them. First, the total amount of finance required by industry will depend on the value of investment undertaken and the amount of retained earnings. The higher the real volume of investment and the faster the growth of real income, the bigger will be the inflow of funds to the institutions, but the bigger also will be the demand for finance. If more finance is provided from retained earnings, this factor will increase the value of shareholders'

---

[6] An example is Roger Opie, 'A Radical Reappraisal', in *The Banker*, February 1977, pp. 101-3.

assets and justify a rise in share prices. Similarly, if the flow of institutional funds is raised by inflation, this will also raise both the money value of new investment and of existing real assets. Provided government refrains from 'counter-inflation' policies that destroy profitability and the incentive to invest, the natural consequences would be both a rise in the amount of finance, in terms of current money, required for new investment and a rise in the share prices to match the rise in the money value of existing assets.

The proportion of new finance raised by equities will also depend on the attractiveness of other sources. Industry can borrow on short and medium term from the banks, and insurance companies and pension funds also provide finance in a variety of ways besides equities. Issues of fixed-interest securities have been small in the recent past, largely because of the demands of the public sector, but at times they have been substantial. The financial institutions provide mortgages, enter into sale and lease-back arrangements on property, put up office and other buildings for leasing, and lease plant and equipment. The institutions are very flexible in the way in which they use their new money, responding to changes in the relative yields of different types of asset and to prospects of capital depreciation.

Finally, the demand for equities from the personal sector may be very different in the future from what it has been in the past. There are difficulties in equity investment for people of small means, though they can be much alleviated by unit trusts, but a relaxation of the pressure on higher incomes could do much to stem the flow of sales by the personal sector.

The bogey-man myth

Both the collective personality of the bogey-man and his bad habits are largely a myth. There are several hundred investing institutions and, though some are much larger than others, the power that even the largest can exert in the equity markets is trivial compared to that of the Bank of England in the gilt-edged market.

The investment behaviour of institutions has been mis-interpreted through some hoary fallacies. There is very little evidence that worthwhile investment has been held back by lack of finance, as the Wilson Committee recorded in its interim report.[7] The low rate of invest-

---

[7] Committee to Review the Functioning of Financial Institutions, *Progress Report on Financing of Industry and Trade,* HMSO, December 1977.

ment in Britain must be attributed primarily to government or party policies that have undermined profitability and destroyed incentives. The London market is not 'over-active' in relation to those of other countries. The allegation that it is arises from the elementary error of ignoring the jobbing system that bargains recorded only once in other centres are 'marked' twice in London. Cyclical movements in prices tend to be of rather wider amplitude but fewer in number in London than in most other centres. Moreover, the wider amplitude can be explained largely in terms of the violence of changes in the economic situation and in government policy. Institutional invest- ment managers, like other sensible people, try to buy as much as possible when economic prospects look good rather than when they look bad, but that is no reason for blaming them for fluctuations that arise, like those of 1974-75 and 1976-77, from government policy.

5. SUMMARY

To sum up: the flow of funds into the long-term institutions is not likely to be very different, in relation to total saving and investment, in the future from what it has been in the past. It is impossible to forecast in detail how that flow will be distributed between different borrowers and different types of lending, but this can safely be left to the market.

The institutions will probably continue to increase their total share in equity ownership, but there is no reason why this process should accelerate; on the contrary, if discouragements to personal savings are reduced, it could slow down. The institutions are far too numerous for any one of them to exercise any significant influence over the market as a whole. Institutional managers behave like other well-informed and sensible people; they will provide finance to potentially profitable enterprises on 'reasonable' terms. They cannot be expected to rush into the market when economic prospects are bad, but this does not mean that they should be blamed for price fluctuations that are due either to external events or to the vacillations of government policy.

The reaction of the Wilson Committee to the threat of the institu- tional bogey-man should be a careful look under the bed; there is nothing very frightening there.

2. The Efficiency of the British Capital Market

R. A. BREALEY

Barclaytrust Professor of Investment,
London Graduate School of Business Studies

City Lights

The Author

RICHARD BREALEY is the Barclaytrust Professor of Investment and the Director of the Institute of Finance and Accounting at the London Graduate School of Business Studies. He is a director of the American Finance Association and an associate editor of the *Journal of Finance, Journal of Financial Economics,* and *Financial Analysts' Journal.* His books include *An Introduction to Risk and Return* (MIT Press, 1969), *Security Prices in a Competitive Market* (MIT Press, 1971), and (with J. Lorie) *Modern Developments in Investment Management* (2nd edition, Dryden Press, 1977).

20

1. INTRODUCTION

Before we decide how well the capital market is doing its job we need to decide exactly what job we *want* it to do. Many of the more fashionable criticisms of the capital market make no sense because they have no consistent criterion for a well-functioning capital market. I therefore begin by discussing the roles of the capital market as a provider of funds for industry and as a mechanism by which individuals can borrow and lend.

Good capital investment decisions require that new funds should always be available at a 'fair' price. I therefore discuss the cost of capital to British industry and examine suggestions that it is unduly high.

Whether the capital market does its job well or badly depends principally on whether it charges a *fair* price for funds. But how can we determine whether a price is 'fair'? Most economists would say that the only meaningful measure of 'fair' is whether prices reflect all the available information in a competitive market. I shall examine how efficiently British security prices reflect information and how far industry can raise new money at these prices.

Many of the well-publicised criticisms of the British capital market are misdirected. Our concern should be not to increase government interference in the capital markets but to remove impediments to competition. In the last section of this article I discuss which parts of the markets are not fully competitive.

2. THE ROLE OF A CAPITAL MARKET

The capital market provides a mechanism for individuals and firms to buy and sell claims on future income. Stocks, shares, mortgages and insurance policies are all examples of such claims. It is often helpful to distinguish between the primary and secondary capital markets. In the primary market new claims are sold for cash and the funds are then used for capital investment. In the secondary market only existing claims are traded and no new cash is made available for investment. Most capital market institutions serve both the primary and the secondary function. The stock market, for example, provides a mechanism whereby a company can sell new shares to finance capital expansion (the primary function) as well as for individual investors to buy and sell existing shares (the secondary function).

The economic benefits of a secondary market

The secondary markets serve an important economic function. They allow an individual to store or anticipate his income. A would-be house buyer, for example, does not need to wait until he accumulates sufficient cash: building societies provide a mechanism whereby he can buy his house by borrowing against his future income. The money for the house purchase comes, of course, from depositors— those who wish to postpone consumption. Both borrower and lender are better off (i.e. happier) than if they were obliged to consume income as it arrived.[1]

The building society is an example of a mechanism whereby individuals can separate the *timing* of their consumption from that of their income. But the secondary market also provides a mechanism whereby they can separate the *risk* of a shortfall in their consumption from that of a shortfall in their income.

The commodity markets, for instance, allow the farmer or the merchant to hedge against the possibility of price fluctuations in his commodity. He expects to pay an insurance premium for getting rid of this risk: the speculator who forms the other side of the bargain expects to *receive* a premium for taking on the risk. Both the hedger and the speculator are better off as a result.

When individuals exchange or trade risk in the capital markets, they do not merely shift the burden from one to another. By spreading risks around they *reduce* the total amount of risk in the economy. All insurance companies are built up on this principle of risk spreading. The risk in an insurance company is borne by the shareholder, but it is far *less* than the sum of the individual risks. In the same way, when an industrial company invests in new plant and equipment the risk is borne by the shareholder but this risk is substantially reduced as long as the shareholder holds a diversified portfolio.[2]

---

[1] One of the first economists to analyse the role of the secondary markets was Irving Fisher [11].

[2] See, for example, Linter [17].

The economic benefits of a primary market

Large companies want large amounts of capital. Inevitably the investment is too large for one individual. The primary capital market provides a mechanism whereby individuals can pool their funds to invest in the same enterprise.

Joint ventures and marriages do not always work. The two partners sometimes find they have different tastes. How then does the professional manager cope when faced with thousands of shareholders with varying attitudes to risk and the length of time they wish to part with their money? Trying to consult their individual tastes would be like trying to run the Greater London Council by town meeting. Fortunately this is not necessary. The miser and spendthrift, the gambler and coward can all conveniently participate in the same enterprise as long as each can use the secondary capital market to adjust the risk and time-pattern of his cash flows. I do not mind ICI investing in 20-year projects as long as I can sell my shares in the stock market, and I do not mind ICI taking rather more risks as long as I can offset them by putting a little more of my money in the building society. The chairman of ICI does not have to consult my individual tastes. All I ask him to do is to maximise the value of my investment. He will do that by accepting any project that offers a return in excess of the return that I could get by investing in the capital market.

Here then we have the ingredients for a successful separation between management and ownership. It will work as long as all companies can raise new funds at a 'fair' price and as long as all investors are able to buy and sell claims in the secondary market at a 'fair' price. Such a system will maximise investor welfare. And as long as each firm prices its goods competitively, it will also lead to optimal investment decisions.

3. FASHIONABLE CRITICISMS OF THE CAPITAL MARKETS

Let us pause at this point to consider a few of the more fashionable criticisms of the basic role of the capital markets.

(1) 'The secondary market syphons off funds'

One of the most patently silly criticisms is that a secondary market syphons off funds that could be used for new capital formation. In its submission to the Wilson Committee, the NEC of the Labour

Party complained that institutional funds were being invested in the secondary market, in agricultural land and works of art, instead of being used to rebuild the country's industrial base. This is a fallacy. If I buy your shares, your land, or your paintings, there is a change in ownership but my action does not alter the total amount of investment in the economy or the nation's wealth one iota.

Samuels, Grove and Goddard have given a slight twist to this argument by complaining that 'in London, people with money find it more profitable to buy and sell shares already traded on the market than to supply that new money to a company'.[3] If we are to believe them, the expected return on new issues is too low rather than too high.

(2) 'Risk sharing is gambling'

It is common to deride activity in the secondary market as socially wasteful gambling. If you and I toss pennies or bet on a racehorse, we are each assuming an unnecessary risk. But when we invest in the stock market, we are not *creating* risk; we are assuming part of the real productive risk in the economy. By sharing this risk as widely as possible the total amount of risk is substantially reduced.

(3) 'Company reliance on retained earnings diminishes the value of a capital market'

Less than 10 per cent of the new funds for investment come from new public issues of equity and debt. The remainder is largely provided by the banks or out of retained earnings. Here is fuel indeed for critics of the capital market. What better evidence that the stock market is failing to provide the funds needed by industry? Instead of getting on with the job of providing capital for new investment it merely provides an 'Overdeveloped secondary market in which investors trade equities between themselves'.

But before the critic's breast bursts with indignation, he should think for a moment. *Given the company's investment policy, and capital structure*, can it make any difference what proportion of the company's money is provided by rights issues?[4] Would we be any better (or worse) off if each company distributed all its earnings as dividends

---

[3] Samuel, Groves, and Goddard [23].

[4] Companies raising new equity capital usually offer the new shares to their existing shareholders. This is known as a rights issue.

and immediately clawed back the additional distribution in the form of a rights issue?[5]

Retained earnings are like compulsory rights issues: in other words they also represent new capital put up by the shareholders. Shareholders are happy to provide capital in the form of retained earnings only so long as they can at any time turn their investment into cash by selling their shares at a 'fair' price in the secondary market. That investors are content to see companies plough back their funds is an indication that the stock market is doing its job. It is ironic that the market should be castigated for the consequences of its success.

(4) 'The capital market misallocates capital'

We said that the firm's dividend policy does not matter, given its investment policy. The more the firm pays out in dividends the more it must recover by rights issues. But suppose that investment policy is not held constant. It is sometimes suggested, for example, that management allocates retained earnings, whereas the stock market allocates the capital provided by rights issues. In this case we would favour high pay-out.or high retained earnings according to whether we believed that investors or managers were the better able to distinguish profitable investment opportunities. Unfortunately this dichotomy ignores the way that security issues work. A company can *always* raise new money by rights issue as long as it offers the new shares below the price of the old shares. Investors do not *allocate* the capital raised by a rights issue: they respond to any offer of shares by buying if they are priced too low or selling if they are priced too high.

It is extremely misleading to speak of the market as 'allocating' capital or of companies as subject to the 'discipline of the market'. The decision to raise and invest cash always belongs to management. There may, however, be behavioural reasons why managers scrutinise projects more closely if they require outside funds. The evidence here is unclear. Several surveys have suggested that managers do require higher returns on money raised by rights issue.[6] On the other hand,

---

[5] The irrelevance of dividend policy, given investment policy and capital structure, was pointed out by Miller and Modigliani [20].

[6] See, for example, Donaldson [5].

econometric studies do not reveal any significant difference between the marginal return on retained earnings and the marginal return on equity raised by rights.[7] And even if we could distinguish such a difference, the policy implications would not be clear. We would have no way of knowing whether managers are (*a*) over-cautious in raising new equity *or* (*b*) unduly liberal in spending retained earnings. In the face of such uncertainty probably the only sensible policy is to leave well alone. That implies a tax system that neither encourages nor discourages dividends (which we have) and freedom from dividend restraint (which we do not).

4. THE COST OF CAPITAL

When a company invests capital in a new project, it incurs an opportunity cost. This cost is the return the funds could be expected to earn if invested in the capital market in a security of comparable risk and duration.

Estimating the cost of capital in the UK

The return on a risk-free security such as Treasury Bills is known and published. Unfortunately, the *Financial Times* cannot publish how much more return is *expected* on risky securities. All we can in practice observe are the differences in return that have resulted in the past. Approximately half the time this risk premium will be higher than investors expected and half the time it will be lower. If we average the risk premium over a sufficiently long period, we should have some measure of the premium that investors expected. For the typical UK share this premium has averaged about 9 per cent between 1919 and 1978.

By considering a very long period we can get a rough idea of the relative cost of safe and risky projects. But the estimate is no more than rough. The return investors expected during the past 50 years could well have been 2 per cent more or less than they realised.[8] We do not know how it has been affected by the high rates of inflation or by changes in the tax system.

We emphasise the difficulty of estimating the cost of capital

---

[7] See, for example, Brealey, Hodges and Capron [3].

[8] The standard error on our estimate of the average risk premium is about ·02.

because some publicity has been given to a NEDO paper in 1975 which purported to show that until the late 1960s the cost of capital was higher for UK companies than for many of their international competitors. We cannot even estimate with much precision the average cost of capital over half a century in the UK.[9] To compare a rate that is expressed in pounds with rates that are expressed in marks or francs we should also need to know the expected change in the exchange rates.[10]

If we want to assess whether the cost of capital in the UK is high or low by world standards, we must rely on indirect evidence. For the post-war period the UK has adopted controls on the export of capital. That it has needed to do so is suggestive that investors expected to achieve higher rates of return overseas. Consistent with this view is the fact that, for much of this period, there existed a covered interest differential in favour of US domestic dollar bills.[11] Thus the very tentative indications are that the UK has in the post-war period maintained a cost of capital that is lower than in other major industrial countries.

The cost of capital is unaffected by capital structure

In the UK, long-term debt accounts for roughly a third of shareholders' funds. This ratio is approximately the same as in the USA but substantially less than in France, West Germany, or Japan.[12] It has been alleged that the comparative lack of debt places UK companies at a competitive disadvantage.

The NEC of the Labour Party, for example, complains of the undue caution displayed in British company capital structures which it attributes to

---

[9] Remember, we need to estimate the return *expected* by investors.

[10] National Economic Development Office [2]. The NEDO estimates were based on a model that assumes a constant expected rate of growth of dividends in perpetuity. Estimated expected growth rate was obtained by fitting a trend line to actual growth rate in share prices and dividends over five years. NEDO ignored the fact that these rates were expressed in different currencies, and the international differences in investment risk.

[11] In other words, in the absence of exchange controls I could earn a higher risk-free sterling return by buying dollars, investing in US Treasury bills and selling my dollar receipts forward.

[12] NB: These rates are customarily expressed in terms of book values. In terms of market values the differences may be rather less marked.

'a pervasive attitude of conservatism in our industrial and financial system which may go far to explain British industry's poor investment performance'.

This is nonsense. Security holders receive the benefits of all corporate cash flows, whether or not they are paid out as interest on debt or dividends on stock. Given these cash flows, the capital structure decision simply affects the way the assets are packaged for distribution and cannot affect the company's risk, its value or the cost of capital.[13] There may be some ways in which the use of debt affects the total cash flows. An increase in gearing, for example, increases the probability of bankruptcy and the real economic costs associated with bankruptcy. Insofar as gearing results in conflicts of interest between bondholders and shareholders, it can again impose some additional costs on the system. But these are trivial effects, and if anything they argue against increased debt. To seek the solution of any country's woes in the corporate capital structure is desperation indeed.

5. THE EFFICIENCY OF THE CAPITAL MARKET

We noted above that welfare will be maximised under a capitalist system only if all companies are able to raise new funds at a 'fair' price and if all investors are able to buy and sell claims in the secondary market at a 'fair' price. A market in which participants can trade at a 'fair' price is usually known as an 'efficient' market.[14]

What are the characteristics of an efficient capital market? Clearly we do not expect investors to possess omniscience. It is easy with hindsight to recognise that British shares were under-priced in December 1974, or that property shares were over-priced in 1973. But we cannot judge efficiency simply by counting investors' mistakes. The relevant test of efficiency is whether prices incorporate all information that is available *at the time*.

Three levels of efficiency

Economists like to envisage three levels of efficiency.

(*a*) A market is said to be 'weak form efficient' if prices reflect all the information that is available in the past sequence of prices. In

---

[13] See Modigliani and Miller [21] and, more recently, Miller [19].

[14] A rigorous definition of market efficiency is given in Fama [7].

such a market future price changes cannot be predicted from past price changes: so the price series follows a random walk.

(*b*) A market is said to be 'semi-strong form efficient' if prices reflect all publicly available information. In such a market it is impossible to devise profitable trading rules that require knowledge of such public information as the latest accounts, the Chairman's annual statement, and so on.

(*c*) Finally, a market is said to be 'strong form efficient' if prices reflect all the information that is known about the article's worth. In this case even the diligent research of professional security analysts is insufficient to produce consistently superior investment returns.

It is unrealistic to suppose that any market will be perfectly efficient. The economist's concept of an efficient market merely represents an ideal against which real markets can be compared. A market is likely to be relatively efficient if there are many participants, information is relatively cheap and there are low trading costs.

Secondary market efficiency

The stock market satisfies most of these conditions. Despite the growth of the institutional investor, share ownership remains highly diffused. Legal obligations on disclosure and the efforts of financial journalists and security analysts ensure that information is widely available. High volume and standardisation result in low trading costs. It is therefore not surprising that empirical studies have found that there are only trivial deviations from the random walk model;[15] that after taking account of dealing costs it is not possible to make superior profits from publicly available information;[16] and that, despite their skills and experience, unit trusts and investment trusts do not achieve above-average performance.[17] This last result is not a sign of incompetence—it is a sign of a competitive and well-functioning market.

---

[15] See, for example, Kendall [15], Dryden [6] and Guy [13].

[16] UK tests of the semi-strong theory include analyses of scrip issues by Firth [10], merger announcements by Franks, Broyles and Hecht [12], and balance-of-trade figures by Brealey [1].

[17] See, for example, Firth [8].

Primary market efficiency

An efficient secondary market enables shareholders to delegate running of the company to a professional manager. As long as the shareholders can adjust the time and risk pattern of their cash flows by dealing at 'fair' prices in the secondary market, the professional manager can ignore their individual tastes and concentrate on the task of maximising the value of the enterprise.

But we also need to be sure that the primary capital market is efficient and that companies can raise new capital at the going price. Some people believe that rights issues are costly, that large offerings of stock depress the price, and that it is impossible to sell stock in a bear market. What are the facts? Paul Marsh has analysed almost 1,000 rights issues between 1962 and 1975.[18] The average price decline over the period of the issue was 0·9 per cent; the decline was no greater for large issues than for small issues; and the decline was no greater after a market fall than after a market rise. Companies, in other words, can always raise substantial sums of new money at about the going rate.

Volatility of the stock market

It is sometimes suggested that:

- (a) a criterion of a well-functioning stock market is one in which prices are stable;
- (b) prices on the London market are excessively unstable;
- (c) this is the result of growing institutional ownership;
- (d) it is also the result of excessive speculation.[19]

Our criterion of an efficient market is not that prices should be stable but that they represent 'fair' value. If new information arrives that causes investors to change their assessment of value, we *want* prices to adjust rapidly to that information. I do not know by what standard share prices in London are judged to be excessively volatile. Before 1973 the volatility of British share prices was similar to that in the USA and somewhat less than in most other major stock markets.[20] Since 1975 volatility has been somewhat higher than in

---

[18] Marsh [18].

[19] Once again, the Labour Party's NEC provides a convenient source of such old wives' tales.

[20] For example, Lessard [16] for pre-1974 comparisons of risk.

most of these stock markets. Some people find it obvious (with hindsight) that the decline of British stock prices during 1973 and 1974 was excessive: the true value of the underlying assets could not possibly have changed by 61 per cent. But is it so obvious? Let us take a simple example. Suppose you have a share that pays a dividend of D. The dividend is expected to grow at a rate g in perpetuity, and investors require a return on the share of r. Its value is $\frac{D}{r-g}$. Now think what happened to interest rates during those two years. Short rates rose from 5 per cent to 13 per cent. If the required return, r, on our share also rose by this amount and the expected growth rate, g, was unchanged, the share value would have fallen substantially.

There has been no general trend in the volatility of British share prices during the past half-century, though there have been several periods in which prices have been unusually volatile.[21] These are 1931-32; 1939-40; and 1974-76. It is as absurd to explain the bear market of 1974 in terms of high institutional ownership as it is to explain the bear market of 1931 in terms of low institutional ownership. Both were the result of a sharp decline in corporate prosperity.

It is equally wrong to associate stock-market volatility with the activities of speculators. There is a well-known theorem in economics that successful speculation is stabilising.* The speculator buys when he believes that prices are below their equilibrium level and sells when he believes they are above.

Many of the accusations of undue volatility or short-term speculation are naïve. Nevertheless we must remain in some measure agnostic. If an investor knows that a security is under-priced, he will receive a larger cash flow per pound of outlay than if he bought any other security. So there is an incentive for him to buy even if he does not believe that the price will return to the correct level. But such gains are relatively slight and the incentive to buy correspondingly weak. It is possible, therefore, that persistent discrepancies between price and value may exist. But if we believe this, our solution should be not to diminish competition but to encourage it. In particular, we should make it easier for investors with superior long-term analysis to capitalise on it. A futures market in ordinary shares or,

---

[21] See, for example, Brealey, Byrne and Dimson [2].

*[Discussed by Professor Yamey in his contribution to this Readings, below, pp. 49–50.—ED.]

much more simply, a traded options market, would go some way towards this objective.[22]

6. SOME GENUINE CONCERNS

I do not wish to suggest that we live in the best of all possible worlds. My worries, however, centre on impediments to competition or on distortions in it that segment the market. I shall now describe some examples.

Tax and regulation

Many of the distortions and frictions in the capital market arise from tax and government regulation. For example, individuals pay higher rates of tax on investment income than they pay on capital gains. So highly taxed individuals hold investments that provide their return largely in the form of capital gains and lowly taxed individuals hold investments that provide their return largely in the form of current income. The capital markets are as a result segmented.[23] This distorts production decisions and leads to sub-optimal portfolio decisions.

The Government imposes a tax penalty on personal saving in the form of a dividend surcharge. At the same time it provides substantial tax advantages to financial intermediation. For example, as long as an individual channels his savings through an approved pension scheme, his dividend income is free of tax. Similarly, savings in the form of a life insurance premium are deductible from personal income tax. So the Government by its tax policy encourages intermediation and then sets up committees which spend much of their time worrying why institutions are becoming so important. These tax advantages to intermediation cause individuals to choose more of particular financial services than they really want, so there is further welfare loss.

The tax and regulatory system also distinguishes between different kinds of financial institution. For example, consider the effect of government regulation and taxation on the banking industry. The

---

[22] In a futures market claims are traded for future delivery. The buyer usually buys on margin; that is, he puts up only part of his purchase price now and the remainder when he takes delivery. In an option market investors can for a small payment acquire an option to buy a share at some future date.

[23] See, for example, Hodges and Schaefer [14].

City has been blamed for the rise and fall of the secondary bank. In fact, the secondary banking phenomenon was largely a legacy of reserve requirements from which the secondary banks were exempt. A potentially more serious long-term threat to the UK banking system comes from the tax exemption of building societies. This reduces the ability of the banks to compete with building societies for deposits; the function of high street banking is being increasingly assumed by the societies.

Market incompleteness

A 'complete' market is one in which it is possible to buy or sell any claim. Lloyds can perhaps be regarded as offering a complete market in which individuals can protect themselves against any combination of circumstances. Other things being equal, market completeness enriches choice and increases welfare. In practice, industrial firms issue a far smaller variety of claims than individuals want. Instead of holding shares and debt, I may wish to hold a claim that pays off in the event of death, another that pays if my car is damaged, and so on. There is no reason in principle why industrial companies could not issue such claims themselves or why I could not get together with a number of individuals to insure one another against personal misfortune. But there would be substantial costs to such activity. It is cheaper for industrial companies to issue standardised equity and debt securities and to have a system of financial intermediaries that hold these securities and repackage them to suit individual needs. Financial intermediation is therefore a direct consequence of a demand for specialised financial services and of high personal costs to arranging such services oneself.

In general, British financial institutions have been very responsive to the demand for specialised services. Nevertheless I suspect that there is scope for still wider choice. There may, for example, well be a latent demand for a claim that pays off in the event of high inflation, or a depreciation of sterling, or a change in tax rates. As long as people are not equally affected by such hazards, there must be some price at which such claims would change hands. Two very simple ways to enlarge individual choice would be to provide facilities for short selling and for trading options. I do not suggest that government should subsidise such innovation, but neither should it reduce welfare by placing obstacles in the way of market completeness.

Small company finance

I have suggested that companies whose stocks are actively traded on the Stock Exchange can raise substantial amounts of new capital at 'fair' prices. If there is a financing problem, it must exist for the smaller company whose stock is not quoted or is very rarely traded. To some extent, the problems of such companies reflect management reluctance to relinquish ownership. There are also fixed expenses to any fund-raising which increase the cost of finance to small companies. As long as these represent genuine economic costs there is no reason why we should be concerned that small companies are at a competitive disadvantage.

It is possible that the cost of new funds for small companies could be reduced by alternative trading arrangements. An over-the-counter market similar to that in the USA, for example, has often been proposed. I doubt that this is the solution. I suspect a more useful development would be to encourage the use of dated securities that lack the unconditional obligation of debt. For example, if payments on participating preference stock were deductible for corporate income tax, such stock might play a rather more important role in small company financing.

Companies that are making their first public issue of stock do so by means of an offer for sale. In other words, the price for the shares is set and applications are invited. Because the price is usually set low to ensure subscriptions, the cost of these new issues is generally very high.[24] There are a number of ways in which this wholly unnecessary cost could be avoided. One of the simplest is to sell such issues by auction or 'tender'.

7. CONCLUSION

I have tried to show that a capital market has two interrelated functions. First, by allowing people to invest their money or to borrow, it enables them to separate the time pattern and the riskiness of their spending from that of their income. Second, it enables people with very different tastes to combine together to provide at a 'fair' price the funds for new capital investment.

Many of the well-voiced criticisms of British capital markets make little sense. For instance:

---

[24] See, for example, Dimson [4].

1. The secondary markets do not syphon funds away from industry.
2. Risk sharing is not gambling.
3. A reliance on retained earnings does not diminish the value of a capital market.
4. The capital market does not 'allocate' capital any more than a supermarket 'allocates' food.
5. There is no evidence that the cost of capital in the UK is higher than in other countries.
6. The cost of capital in the UK would not be reduced by increased gearing.
7. Volatility does not indicate an inefficient securities market.
8. There is no evidence that increased volatility is a consequence of increased institutional share-ownership.

Our criterion for the efficiency of the British capital market should be the extent to which securities are 'fairly' priced. Prices are 'fair' when capital markets are competitive; they are likely to be 'unfair' when markets are not competitive. If we wish to improve the operation of the capital market we should seek to remove government or institutional impediments to competition rather than to devise new impediments.

REFERENCES

[1] R. A. Brealey, 'The Distribution and Independence of Successive Rates of Return in the UK Equity Market', *Journal of Business Finance*, 2 (Summer 1970), pp. 29-40.

[2] R. A. Brealey, J. Byrne, E. Dimson, 'The Variability of Market Returns', *Investment Analyst*, 52 (December 1978), pp. 19-23.

[3] R. A. Brealey, S. D. Hodges, D. Capron, 'The Return on Alternative Sources of Finance', *Review of Economics and Statistics*, 58 (November 1976), pp. 469-477.

[4] E. Dimson, 'The Pricing of Unseasoned New Issues', Proceedings of the Conference on Inflation and Capital Markets, IIM, Berlin (January 1977).

[5] G. Donaldson, *Corporate Debt Capacity,* Harvard Business School, 1961.

[6] M. M. Dryden, 'A Statistical Study of UK Share Prices', *Scottish Journal of Political Economy,* 17 (November 1970), pp. 369-389.

[7] E. F. Fama, 'Efficient Capital Markets: A Review of Theory and Empirical Work', *Journal of Finance,* 25 (May 1970), pp. 383-417.

[8] M. A. Firth, 'The Performance of UK Unit Trusts in the Period 1965-1975', Unpublished paper, 1976.

[9] M. A. Firth, 'The Incidence and Impact of Capitalisation Issues', Institute of Chartered Accountants in England and Wales Research Committee Occasional Paper No. 3, 1974.

[10] M. A. Firth, 'The Impact of Earnings Announcements on the Share Price Behaviour of Similar Type Firms', *Economic Journal,* Vol. 86 (1976), pp. 296-306.

[11] I. Fisher, *The Theory of Interest,* Reprint, Augustus M. Kelley, New York, 1975.

[12] J. Franks, J. E. Broyles, M. J. Hecht, 'An Industry Study of the Profitability of Mergers in the United Kingdom', *Journal of Finance,* 32 (December 1977).

[13] J. R. F. Guy, 'The Stock Exchange, London: An Empirical Analysis of Monthly Data from 1960 to 1970', *European Finance Association 1975 Proceedings,* North Holland, 1976.

[14] S. D. Hodges, S. M. Schaefer, 'Tax Rules for Unsegmented Markets', Working paper IFA-28-76, Institute of Finance and Accounting, London Business School, 1976.

[15] M. G. Kendall, 'The Analysis of Economic Time Series, Part I', *Journal of the Royal Statistical Society,* 96 (1953), pp. 11-25.

[16] D. R. Lessard, 'International Diversification', *Financial Analysts Journal,* 32 (Jan.-Feb. 1976), pp. 32-38.

[17] J. Linter, 'Security Prices, Risk, and the Maximal Gains from Diversification', *Journal of Finance,* 20 (December 1965), pp. 587-616.

[18] P. R. Marsh, 'An Analysis of Equity Rights Issues on the London Stock Exchange', Unpublished PhD dissertation, London Business School (April 1977).

[19] M. H. Miller, 'Debt and Taxes', *Journal of Finance*, 32 (May 1977), pp. 261-276.

[20] M. H. Miller, F. Modigliani, 'Dividend Policy, Growth, and the Valuation of Shares', *Journal of Business,* 34 (October 1961), pp. 411-433.

[21] F. Modigliani, M. H. Miller, 'The Cost of Capital, Corporation Finance, and the Theory of Investment', *American Economic Review,* 48 (June 1958), pp. 261-297.

[22] National Economic Development Office, *Finance for Investment,* 1975.

[23] J. M. Samuels, R. E. V. Groves, C. S. Goddard, *Company Finance in Europe,* The Institute of Chartered Accountants in England and Wales, 1975.

3. Commodity Futures Markets, Hedging and Speculation

B. S. YAMEY

Professor of Economics,
University of London
(*London School of Economics*)

The Author

B. S. YAMEY was born in 1919 in Cape Town, South Africa, and graduated at the University of Cape Town. After teaching at Rhodes University, Grahamstown, and at the University of Cape Town, he joined the staff of the London School of Economics (University of London) in December 1947, where he has remained except for a year at McGill University, Montreal. Appointed Professor of Economics in January 1960. Member of the Monopolies and Mergers Commission, 1966-78. Elected a Fellow of the British Academy, 1977.

Professor Yamey's publications include *The Economics of Resale Price Maintenance* (1954); (with P. T. Bauer) *The Economics of Under-developed Countries* (1957); (with R. B. Stevens) *The Restrictive Practices Court* (1965); (ed.) *Economics of Industrial Structure* (1973); (jt. ed.) *Economics of Retailing* (1973); (with B. A. Goss) *Economics of Futures Trading* (1976); and articles on the history and economics of distribution; the economics and law of monopoly and restrictive practices; commodity markets and futures exchanges; less developed countries; and the history of accounting.

Professor Yamey is a member of the Advisory Council of the IEA. He wrote its first Hobart Paper, *Resale Price Maintenance and Shopper's Choice,* in 1960 (4th Edition, 1964).

1. SIZE AND SCOPE

The organised futures markets 'make a substantial contribution to our invisible earnings, estimated in a recent Bank of England *Review* (March 1977) to be of the order of £200 million a year'.[1] They are an important element in the extensive network of City institutions. A large volume of business is voluntarily transacted in these privately-organised markets, by both domestic and foreign producers, traders, processors and manufacturers.

Chicago, London and New York are the three major international centres of futures trading. The commodities traded in London futures markets include several metals (copper, lead, tin, zinc, silver and aluminium), rubber, sugar, coffee, cocoa, wool, barley, wheat, palm oil and soya bean meal. The corresponding lists for New York or Chicago are longer, in part the consequence of the larger United States domestic market. Nevertheless, for several commodities, such as copper, which are the subject of futures trading both in London and also in New York or Chicago, the London market is accepted as being the more important and it attracts more international business.

2. EVOLUTION AND INNOVATION IN FUTURES TRADING

A market institution organised on a voluntary basis emerges or evolves because it can provide required services or facilities more efficiently than existing arrangements or because it can provide new services or facilities for which there turns out to be an unsatisfied but adequate demand. Typically, the improvements provided by new market institutions or arrangements derive from the more efficient generation, dissemination and utilisation of market information they make possible and the more efficient and reliable methods of transacting business they permit. They prosper only to the extent that they yield such benefits to individuals or firms which are perfectly free to by-pass them and to make their transactions however and

---

[1] House of Lords, Select Committee on Commodity Prices, *Report of the Committee,* HMSO, 1977, vol. 1, para. 8.28.

wherever they please. This is as true of the medieval fairs of Champagne or the village markets of Nigeria as it is of trading in futures on the London Metal Exchange.[2]

Standardised contract

The central innovation in futures trading, which originated in the 19th century (although some aspects of it can be traced before then), is the concentration of dealing on a highly standardised contract which is traded subject to carefully devised rules and safeguards. The contract abstracts from the peculiarities of quality and condition and the specificities of place and time which cannot be ignored in dealings in the actual commodity (the 'actuals' or 'physicals'). By virtue of this concentration of dealing and standardisation of subject-matter, trading in futures contracts can take place with low transaction costs and without inspection of the goods.

Together with standardisation of contracts there has developed in futures markets a system of guaranteeing the performance of contractual undertakings which is virtually watertight. The usual method is for a clearing house owned by or associated with the market organisation to guarantee the execution of contracts, and for it to safeguard its own financial position by limiting trading to principals of financial substance and by requiring periodically adjusted deposits or margins against open contracts.[3] In consequence, the individual principal (and the clients for whom he acts) need not be concerned with the identity or reliability of those with whom he enters into futures contracts. Futures trading is impersonal trading; transaction costs are further reduced; and the risks of default are virtually eliminated. The market is widened and becomes more continuous; and a contract traded in an active futures market has a high degree of liquidity. These are all features in respect of which a futures

---

[2] A discussion of the reasons why futures trading exists for some commodities but not others is in B. A. Goss and B. S. Yamey (eds.), *The Economics of Futures Trading*, Macmillan, 1976, Editorial Introduction, pp. 44-5; see also L. G. Telser and H. N. Higinbotham, 'Organised Futures Markets: Costs and Benefits', *Journal of Political Economy*, October 1977.

[3] In American futures markets, limits on daily price movements further protect the clearing house.
   The reasons why the London Metal Exchange does not have a clearing house are discussed in House of Lords, *Report, op. cit.*, para. 8.24. Since this Report was published, the Exchange has instituted a system for monitoring the trading positions of its members.

contract is superior to a contract in physicals, whether it is for current delivery (cash or spot) or for delivery at some future date (forward). They explain why futures contracts are used for hedging.

3. THE ECONOMICS OF HEDGING

Suppose a business man has to hold a quantity of a commodity in the course of carrying on his business: he requires a stock so as to ensure continuity in his operations, whether these are merchanting, processing or manufacturing. He is at risk in the sense that the price of the commodity may fall while he is holding his stock. He can avoid this risk by making forward sales in the actuals market. If this course is followed, he has to find buyers for his particular variety or quality of the commodity (or of the product to be manufactured from it), negotiate prices and settle questions of time, place and circumstances of delivery. In this respect, trade in the market for the physical commodity (compared with the market for futures) has some of the limitations and disabilities of barter (compared with trade).[4] Moreover, there is the cost of ascertaining the creditworthiness of buyers and the risk of default. And stock sold forward may have to be ear-marked and so no longer be available to meet unforeseeable requirements as these may arise.

Benefits of a futures market

Where there is a futures market a different course is open to him. He can hedge the stock he holds by selling an appropriate quantity of futures contracts. This alternative avoids some of the difficulties associated with the forward selling of actuals, and the necessary transactions can be executed quickly and cheaply and without risk of default. Moreover, the hedged stock remains freely available to meet requirements as and when they materialise.

Take another example of hedging. Suppose market expectations about future supplies and requirements relative to current supply and demand conditions are such as to warrant an increase of stock holding. A trader can act accordingly by buying actuals and waiting; but then he is exposed to the risk of a fall in price should his and the market's expectations turn out to have been wrong. Or he can buy a stock of actuals and simultaneously make an actuals contract for

---

[4] Telser and Higinbotham, *op. cit.*, p. 970.

forward delivery with a buyer willing to pay a price which justifies the cost of carrying the additional stock; but then he is likely to have high costs in seeking out and negotiating with a buyer interested in his particular stock of the commodity, and there are the risks of default. If there is a futures market, however, he can acquire supplies and hedge them by a sale of futures contracts. Given the assumed state of market expectations, futures will be priced at a suitably attractive premium above the current price of actuals; and the premium of the forward futures price over the spot actuals price will cover the cost of storing the commodity. Transaction costs are low; default risk is zero; and the risk of price change is avoided.[5]

Although every futures contract specifies delivery of the subject-matter, and if held to its maturity will entail such delivery, in most active futures markets only a small proportion of traded contracts is in practice settled by actual delivery. However useful it is for hedging purposes, the typical futures contract is not a useful instrument for effecting delivery. This is so because the typical contract gives the seller one or several delivery options. He can usually choose from among a stipulated range of grades or qualities to deliver; from among a range of places at which to deliver; and from among a range of dates on which to deliver (sometimes any day within a stated month).

The extent of delivery options open to the seller differs among commodities: they tend to be widest for agricultural commodities and narrowest for non-ferrous metals. Nevertheless, the presence of any seller's options means that a futures contract is not normally a suitable instrument through which a buyer can assure himself of receiving exactly what he requires when and where he requires it.

Seller's options reduce risk of market manipulation

These seller's options, which help to differentiate actuals contracts from futures contracts, have been introduced largely to reduce, indeed almost to eliminate, the risk of market manipulation through the purchase of futures, cornering deliverable supplies and squeezing

---

[5] A more detailed discussion of hedging in futures is in H. Working, 'Futures Trading and Hedging', *American Economic Review,* June 1953, and 'New Concepts Concerning Futures Markets', *American Economic Review,* June 1962, and in Goss and Yamey, *op. cit.,* pp. 17-29. Working's major papers on futures markets are conveniently reprinted in *Selected Writings of Holbrook Working,* Chicago Board of Trade, 1977.

those who have delivery obligations to discharge as sellers of maturing or matured futures. The options do not, however, embarrass those who use futures markets. As a rule neither party at the time of making the contract intends to discharge his obligations on it by making or taking physical delivery. The hedger finds it more efficient to sell his particular supplies in the actuals market, where their peculiarities of quality, condition, time and place can be expected to be more fully reflected in price, rather than to deliver them on the standardised futures contract (even if his supplies should be eligible for delivery). The speculator who buys or sells futures in the expectation of a favourable price movement is also not interested in taking or making delivery. Instead, the obligations on most futures contracts are discharged by off-setting purchases or sales of like-dated contracts—with price differences being settled through the clearing-house. But the condition that delivery can be insisted upon by either party to an open futures contract serves to link the prices of futures quite firmly to the corresponding prices of actuals. And this in turn makes possible the practice of hedging in futures by keeping the two sets of prices more or less in line.[6]

Long hedging

Hedging has been considered so far as the sale of futures to balance or cover a holder of a stock of the commodity: such a hedger is long in actuals and short in futures, and is known as a short hedger. There is also long hedging: a trader or manufacturer with a commitment to deliver the commodity (or its product) at some future date covers his short actuals position by the purchase of futures. Typically, the volume of short hedging exceeds the volume of long hedging by wide margins.[7] Therefore non-hedging operators in futures, called speculators, are necessary if the market is to accommodate hedging. But even if the volumes of short and long hedging were about equal, a futures market made up solely of hedgers would be less efficient for hedging than one which also included speculators. Their presence

---

[6] A commitment in actuals hedged in the futures market is subject to the risk of unpredictable changes in the relative prices of a futures contract and of the grade, etc. of the actuals in which the commitment is made. This risk is generally much smaller than the risk of changes in the price of the actuals.

[7] A more detailed discussion is in B. S. Yamey, 'Short Hedging and Long Hedging in Futures Markets', *Journal of Law and Economics*, April 1971.

serves to widen the market, to make trading more continuous and hence to enable hedges to be placed and lifted more readily and with less cost; that is, it serves to increase the liquidity of futures contracts. The wider and more continuous the market, the smaller the effect on price of any given volume of sales or purchases by hedgers. Moreover, speculators serve to link prices between the various futures markets in the same commodity, and also between the various contract maturities for the same commodity.

4. THE ROLE OF SPECULATION

Even critics of futures trading recognise the services provided by speculators in facilitating hedging by those who have a (so-called) 'legitimate' business interest in the commodity. And one highly oversimplified view of the activities of speculators is that they do no more (or little more) than supply price-insurance services to hedgers and earn profits as a reward. They take on risks which merchants and manufacturers want to shed, and are willing to shed at some cost to themselves.[8]

Advocates of futures trading, while acknowledging the role of speculators in connection with hedging, make a wider claim for speculators and speculation. It is that speculation improves the process of price formation in the markets for the commodities traded; and that facilities for futures trading increase the volume, lower the 'price' and improve the quality of the services performed by speculators in the formation of prices. In a nutshell, the claim is that speculation in futures causes prices to respond more readily and accurately to changes in market conditions and prospects; or, in other words,

---

[8] This influential but misleading interpretation of hedging and speculation is associated with J. M. Keynes and his hypothesis of 'normal backwardation'. According to this theory, in a market in which short hedging preponderates the prices of forward-dated futures tend to be below the eventual prices of the same futures when they reach maturity. It follows that speculators (i.e. non-hedgers), who would be net long in futures, would make profits. The theory is critically examined and found deficient in C. S. Rockwell, 'Normal Backwardation, Forecasting, and the Returns to Commodity Futures Traders', *Food Research Institute Studies,* 1967, Supplement to Vol. VII; and in Goss and Yamey, *op. cit.,* pp. 31-2.

that fluctuations in price are *reduced* through the more timely and better informed actions of speculators.

The risk-taking speculator and the futures market

All decisions committing resources to an uncertain future are speculative; and speculation is therefore inherent and ineradicable in a world of change. A merchant or manufacturer long or short in actuals and not hedging his position fully is acting as a speculator. Specialisation in speculative activity may be expected to improve the quality of decisions taken, especially if it is the resources of the speculators which are placed at risk by the decisions. Such specialists may be expected to inform themselves of likely developments affecting the outcome of their decisions and, by specialisation, to acquire and use relevant skills. This description of the speculative function is indeed the basis of the argument of Adam Smith that the speculative corn dealer improves the intra-seasonal allocation of a harvest and so acts, albeit unwittingly, in the interests of consumers of the corn.[9] Smith wrote before futures markets had come into existence.

Futures trading promotes the specialisation of the speculative function by freeing the speculator from merchanting or manufacturing involvement in the commodity in question; by guaranteeing contracts and so freeing the speculator from the need to assess risks other than price risks; and by reducing transaction costs. It widens the market for speculative activities and it facilitates the division of labour between speculation and other activities concerning the commodity. Since Adam Smith identified the interrelated widening of markets and increasing division of labour as powerful engines of economic advance, he would no doubt have welcomed the development of futures trading. He might well have approved this statement by Alfred Marshall about speculation in futures markets:[10]

> 'On the whole it seems safe to conclude that, since those who buy because their investigations lead them to think that the supply is likely to run short, or sell because they are convinced it has been underrated,

---

[9] Adam Smith, *The Wealth of Nations,* 1776, Book 4, Chapter 5, section b. The subject is discussed also by John Stuart Mill, *Principles of Political Economy,* 1848, Book 4, Chapter 2, sections 4 and 5.

[10] Alfred Marshall, *Industry and Trade,* Macmillan, 1919, Book 2, Chapter 5, section 4.

will gain if they are right and lose if they are wrong;[11] therefore they are in their own interest contributing to the public the best judgement of minds that are generally alert, well-informed and capable. Their influence certainly tends to lessen the amplitude of price variations from place to place and from year to year.'[12]

Yet there is a widespread belief that speculation tends to aggravate and increase price fluctuations over time, and that this tendency is more pronounced in commodities with futures trading. Beliefs about destabilising speculation lay behind, for example, the closure by government of cotton futures trading in Liverpool after the Second World War, of several futures markets in India, and of the onions futures market in the United States.

Marshall qualified his statement, quoted above, by referring to 'the evil side of such speculations'. What he had in mind was 'abuse by unscrupulous men, aided as they often are by the folly of ill-informed speculators'. As to abuse by market manipulators, the contract rules and the powers of the market authorities are today such that deliberate manipulation of prices or market information is likely to be rare and the chances of success small. (And, of course, these practices are possible on markets without futures trading.) As to ill-informed speculators, by which description Marshall was referring to 'amateur speculators', it is evident that just as the operations of a futures market facilitate speculation by informed specialists or 'professionals', so they facilitate speculation by apparently uninformed amateurs, particularly as both transaction costs and initial outlays are modest.

---

[11] Specialist speculators in futures markets typically do not handle or stock the commodity. Their bullishness (or bearishness) does, however, affect accumulation (or decumulation) of stocks through its effect on the difference (positive or negative) between the forward futures price and the current actuals price and hence on the incentives to merchants to increase or decrease their hedged stock-holdings.

[12] The analysis of Marshall and others implies that speculative activities are profitable to the speculators only when they serve to stabilise prices. It has been shown in theoretical papers that speculation can be profitable when it is destabilising in the sense that the variance of prices is increased: M. Farrell, 'Profitable Speculation', *Economica,* May 1966; and J. Schimmler, 'Speculation, Profitability, and Price Stability—A Formal Approach', *Review of Economics and Statistics,* February 1973. These theoretical papers unfortunately do not provide recipes telling speculators how to make money by engaging in destabilising activities.

The participation of amateurs, whatever else it does, also serves to widen the market, increase the continuity of trading on it, and so enhance the liquidity of futures contracts. It is difficult if not impossible to determine by direct inquiry whether it impairs rational price formation and enhances price fluctuations, if only because the term 'amateur' eludes precise definition.

Speculation tends to be stabilising

A number of statistical studies suggest, however, that futures trading (including, that is, the activities of speculators both professional and amateur) tends to reduce price fluctuations, as Marshall claimed. Studies have been made comparing price fluctuations in a period in which there was futures trading with price fluctuations in an earlier, or in a few instances, later period in which there was no futures trading in the commodity. These studies show that performance was usually better (and never worse) in the futures-trading period than in the control period. These tests are not perfect, since the effects of other influences bearing on price performance may have been different in the two periods and so have affected the comparison. But the likelihood of serious or systematic distortions is small, as the studies typically involve comparisons between relatively short and contiguous periods.[13]

A further class of evidence is available. Most suggestions or allegations that speculation in futures markets increases price fluctuations are based on the idea that the professionals, instead of off-setting the effects of ill-informed trading activities of amateurs, find it more profitable to go along with prevailing or developing price trends and so reinforce them. Professional speculators are apt to act in this way, so it is argued, because they believe that they will be able to time the liquidation of their positions profitably before

---

[13] For examples, H. Working, 'Price Effects of Futures Trading', *Food Research Institute Studies,* February 1960; R. W. Gray, 'Onions Revisited', *Journal of Farm Economics,* May 1963; and A. S. Naik, *Effects of Futures Trading on Prices,* Asia Publishing House, 1970. A more elaborate study is in C. C. Cox, 'Futures Trading and Market Information', *Journal of Political Economy,* December 1976.

An interesting experiment in which students acted as 'traders' had as its outcome that speculative trading was stabilising to a high degree: R. M. Miller, C. R. Plott and V. L. Smith, 'Intertemporal Competitive Equilibrium: An Empirical Study of Speculation', *Quarterly Journal of Economics,* November 1977.

the bubble bursts, being able to rely on their continuous contact with the market and their superior appreciation of the underlying supply and demand factors to get out before the amateurs.[14]

If this sort of trading behaviour were common, however, its results would show up in statistical analyses of price changes. A variety of statistical tests has been applied to price series for a number of futures markets, mostly but not exclusively in the United States. The futures markets studied have emerged rather well from the searching tests applied to them. The studies reveal little evidence of the kind of price patterns which would be present if movement trading were a frequent and prominent feature of futures trading. And some of the observed deviations from the hypothesised randomness can be attributed not to the activities of speculators but to such influences as the presence of transaction costs, the operation of official price supports, the prescription of limits on daily price changes, or the occasional thinness of markets.[15]

---

[14] Such an explanation is offered in H. S. Irwin, 'The Nature of Risk Assumption in the Trading on Organised Exchanges', *American Economic Review,* June 1937. Irwin wrote, for example, that speculators engaged in trading on price movements 'are little concerned over what [price] levels are justified by the prevailing situation. They are interested rather in how far other traders will push the movement in prices which they are following at the time' (p. 270).

The House of Lords Select Committee (*Report, op. cit.,* para. 18.2) summarised the views expressed to it by witnesses: 'The nearest to a consensus which emerges from the evidence is that in normal times speculation is probably a stabilising factor. But if there are strong independent causes of major swings, speculation may add to rather than reduce their scale'. The second sentence seems to imply that speculators, in such circumstances, may base their trading decisions on the prevailing price movements rather than on their independent assessments of underlying supply and demand factors.

[15] For reviews and discussions of the issues and results see A. E. Peck (ed.), *Selected Writings on Future Markets,* Chicago Board of Trade, 1977, Editor's Introduction to Section 4, pp. 253-5; Goss and Yamey, *op. cit.,* pp. 34-36, 48; and G. W. Smith, 'Commodity Instability and Market Failure: A Survey of Issues', in F. G. Adams and S. A. Klein (eds.), *Stabilizing World Commodity Markets,* Lexington Books, 1978, pp. 161-7.

It is symptomatic of much modern economics that the standard against which actual market performance tends to be judged is one which it is not possible to attain in practice. The more stringent of the statistical tests are based on the assumptions that there are no costs in making transactions and that the market adjusts instantaneously to any new piece of market information. (If the latter condition were satisfied, it would not be worthwhile for any market operator to incur cost or effort in the search for new market information.)

5. FUTURES TRADING AND PRICE FLUCTUATIONS

Futures trading flourishes best for commodities whose prices are liable to significant fluctuations because of frequent imperfectly predictable changes in supply and demand conditions. In such circumstances there is likely to be an extensive demand for hedging facilities. In practice, futures markets generally operate successfully only if there is a considerable hedging interest. And the attention of speculators is stimulated by the opportunities to profit from the correct forecasting of price changes. The co-existence of significant price fluctuations and active futures trading is not evidence, of course, that the latter causes or intensifies the former.

Importance of 'visible' price variations in futures markets

Futures trading in an active market, it should be added, is subject to numerous transient variations in price: there are apt to be small minute-to-minute changes in price in a market in which all transactions relate to a highly-standardised subject-matter. This 'nervousness' of prices is visible because trading takes place openly and deals are recorded publicly. But this price variability is distinct from, and unconnected with, longer-term price changes or movements. Similar price variations are naturally not so visible for transactions in a physical commodity. These transactions are not standardised, but are affected by the particularities (including reliability) of the parties involved, and their terms and prices are usually not recorded publicly.

Indeed, because of the unusual visibility, clarity and lack of ambiguity of prices in futures markets (as compared with prices in physical commodity transactions), these markets have a valuable economic rôle as sources of price signals which can readily be seen, interpreted and acted upon not only by those who trade in futures but also by others, such as primary producers, who typically do not enter into futures contracts.

The general finding that futures trading tends to reduce price fluctuations rather than to intensify them serves to undermine the occasional contention that bullish speculation in futures has been responsible for the aggravation of spurts of inflation. In any case, the linking of changes in the prices of internationally-traded commodities with changes in the rate of domestic inflation rests upon a simplistic view of the economics of inflation, and one which cannot account *inter alia* for major differences in rates of inflation in different countries.

Could government do better than futures markets?

The delivery date of the most distant futures contract which can be traded in a particular market depends upon the needs of users of the market, primarily those of hedgers. It is in practice unusual for traded futures contracts to have delivery dates as much as two years ahead of the date of trading. (It is three months for copper and tin, eighteen months for sugar.) Hence futures trading cannot directly exercise its favourable effects on price formation much beyond the current and succeeding season in the case of seasonally-produced commodities, and for shorter periods in that of other commodities. Given the political and economic uncertainties surrounding the demand for and supply of commodities (and also of national currencies), it is not surprising that the favourable effects of private speculative and trading activity have a limited time-span. But, with these uncertainties, it is difficult to visualise more effective alternative arrangements.

To many it may seem as if government action is called for. However, the history of governmental and inter-governmental attempts to stabilise prices of particular commodities over longer periods than two years—or for that matter over shorter periods than that—points to the extremely low probability that such alternative or additional arrangements would improve upon the pricing performance of futures markets. In any event, such alternatives would necessarily involve speculation, and speculation on a frighteningly large scale, by a single decision-taker. Speculative decisions would be taken by an individual or a committee whose own resources would not be put in jeopardy by them, who would be subject to direct or indirect political pressures, and who could not be expected to have relevant skills and insights beyond the reach of private speculators.

6. THE FUTURE FOR FUTURES

Commodity futures markets are part and parcel of the network of City institutions. They link up directly with financial institutions. For example, hedged stocks generally are better collateral for borrowing than unhedged stocks, so that the cost of finance to merchants, processors and manufacturers is reduced. Again, because of their liquidity and of the system of trading on deposits and margins, futures contracts are candidates for inclusion in investment portfolios. Moreover, the very functioning of the markets and clearing-houses involves the handling of large sums of money.

Recent developments, notably in the United States, have brought futures trading in even more intimate contact with financial markets. In Chicago, futures trading in interest rates was introduced a few years ago. Futures contracts based respectively on certain mortgage-backed certificates guaranteed by the Government National Mortgage Association (the so-called Ginny-Maes) and on certain treasury bills permit hedging and speculation in interest rates. In Chicago, also, there is active futures trading in foreign currencies including sterling, German marks, Swiss francs and Mexican pesos —and further currencies as well as Euro-dollars are expected to be added to the list. The post-war economic environment has created a large demand for the new facilities provided, and the standardisation of contracts and the clearing-house guaranteeing of contract performance are major attractive features of these new financial instruments.

Even more interesting developments are under discussion. It is quite likely that, subject to the necessary authorisation by the official Commodity Futures Trading Commission, which is the regulatory agency in the United States, futures trading in share price indexes may soon be organised in the United States, as is already the case in Amsterdam. There is talk, also, of a futures contract based on some general price index: certainly, such indexes of inflation now have enough movement to encourage sizeable hedging and speculative interests.[16]

---

[16] In a paper published a few years ago (M. C. Lovell and R. C. Vogel, 'A CPI-Futures Market', *Journal of Political Economy,* July/Aug. 1973), the authors considered the possibility of extending 'the concept of a futures market to provide a means of hedging against fluctuations in the general price level, as measured by the market basket with which the [United States] Bureau of Labor Statistics constructs the consumer price index'. They suggested that such a futures market would ease the task of adapting to the uncertainties of inflation, and also provide useful information on expectations about future changes in the price level.

It should be apparent that the possibility of delivery in settlement of a general price index futures contract (or of a share price index contract) is virtually excluded.

One advantage of a *general* price index contract is that speculators need not concern themselves with the details of market conditions for particular goods or services (or particular shares), but can base their trading decisions on their views about *general* market developments. Moreover, it is very much easier with such contracts to give expression to bearish views.

The post-war increase in the volume of futures trading and the widening of the range of contracts traded in the United States have been impressive. In part they have been due to the enterprise and initiative of a few futures-market organisations, notably the Chicago Board of Trade and the Chicago Mercantile Exchange. Their example in the development of new futures contracts may well be emulated elsewhere.

4. The International Money and Capital Markets

PAUL BAREAU

Economic Adviser,
International Publishing Corporation

The Author

PAUL BAREAU graduated at the London School of Economics and is now a Fellow of the LSE. Most of his working life has been devoted to financial journalism. In this capacity he served the *Financial News,* the *News Chronicle,* the *Daily Mail* and the *Statist* of which he was editor between 1961 and 1967. He is now economic adviser to the International Publishing Corporation. He acts as economic consultant to Barclays Bank. He is a director of three investment trusts. He is a regular contributor to the *Journal of the Institute of Bankers.* During the war he was a member of the UK Treasury delegation in Washington. In that capacity he worked on the Bretton Woods projects and was a member of the UK delegation at the first meeting of Governors of the World Bank and International Monetary Fund held in Savannah in 1946.

1. THE GROWTH OF EUROCURRENCY MARKETS

The dominant and fundamental feature in the evolution of the international money and capital markets over the past two decades has been the growth of the multi-national, multi-currency markets to which the prefix 'Euro' has come to be applied, mistakenly, because it gives them a European connotation which does much less than justice to their truly *world-wide* membership and operation.

'Euro' currencies are deposited with banks located outside the countries by which they are issued and for which these countries are responsible. But it is self-evident that for every such 'offshore' deposit there must be, at the end of the line of re-depositors, a deposit with a bank in the country of the currency's origin. A Euro-dollar deposit, for example, arising out of the dollar proceeds of exports from Germany to the United States but invested with a bank in London, has as its counterpart the London bank's deposit with the US bank through which the payment was made. This simple triangular transaction may be intricately complicated by the velocity with which the original Euro-deposit subsequently changes hands; but in the long, ultimate run, after all double, treble, quadruple, . . . counting has been eliminated, this clear relationship between the domestic and the 'Euro' currency remains.

The currencies so deposited, then lent and re-lent in offshore markets, are those in which international commercial and financial operations are, in the main, transacted: US dollars, German marks, Swiss francs, sterling, Dutch guilders, French francs, but with US dollars claiming over 70 per cent of the total amount currently outstanding.

Origin: 1958 IMF convertibility

There have been instances of foreign currency deposits with domestic banks stretching back into the 19th century, but the origin of a market in external, offshore deposits such as we know today can be said to date from 1958, when the major member countries of the International Monetary Fund (IMF) decided to make their currencies freely convertible for non-residents. The shackles of exchange control may have continued to grip the operations of residents in some of these countries; but for non-residents the freedom, essential to the development and functioning of an international capital market, was restored.

The use made of that freedom is inscribed in the figures collected by the Bank for International Settlements (BIS) and as far as possible corrected for multiple counting of inter-bank re-depositing. From negligible figures in 1958 the external currency assets of banks in the Group of Ten countries[1] had, by 30 June 1978, grown to the equivalent of $400,000 million. With the comparable assets of branches of US banks in offshore banking centres in the Caribbean and the Far East, the total swells to $733,000 million. These figures must be corrected for double counting, but are a token of what freedom can achieve when a market is given the opportunity to develop undeterred by the inhibitions of exchange control.

2. US RESTRICTIONS AND THE BIRTH OF THE EURODOLLAR

Why and how were those first hesitant steps taken? What were the forces that fed this expansion to well-nigh unimaginable figures? Where is the business done?

The markets as they now exist and with the dominant importance they command are the product of the co-existence of restrictions on the flow of funds in some spheres and corresponding freedom in others. And since the dollar has been and is likely to remain the principal currency dealt in, the paradox can best be illustrated by the United States.

The restrictions were on the outflow of capital which began with the Interest Equalisation Tax in 1963 and led in 1965 to the Foreign Credit Restraint Guidelines, voluntary at first, then mandatory, and the controls over direct investment abroad by US corporations. Those official restrictions had the inevitable effect of driving external dollar business away from the domestic market. But they were abetted by another kind of restriction, which pre-dated the official measures: the regulation which limited how much US banks could pay on deposits (Regulation Q). This restriction was matched on the other side of the balance sheet by rigidity in rates charged for loans

---

[1] USA, Canada, UK, West Germany, France, Italy, Belgium, Holland, Japan, Sweden.

and by the increase in the true cost of borrowing following the rule of American banks to demand a proportionate re-depositing of the proceeds of a loan into a non-interest bearing current or cheque account.

Countervailing freedom for non-residents

The countervailing freedom was the international, virtually uncontrolled freedom of capital movements for non-residents, which reigned from 1958 onwards when the major member countries of the IMF decided to make their currencies fully convertible for non-residents. Immediately the basis was laid for the development of an international money and capital market, in which operations would be unhampered by exchange and other restrictions.

The Euro-markets—money and bonds—which thus developed were therefore the progenies of decidedly contrasting but not necessarily incompatible parents. And, as in other instances of mixed blood, conceived out of legalised, recognised wedlock, these bastards have grown sturdy and resilient.

'Marxist' beginnings

Among the mixed parentage of these markets, and in particular of the Euro-dollar market, one can also detect Communist bloc fear—that dollar balances held in US banks would be blocked. There can be no doubt that, during and after the Korean war, and following the blocking of some Chinese balances, the State banking organisations in the USSR tended to keep their dollar balances with banks outside the United States. Indeed, it has been suggested that one of these institutions, the Banque Commerciale pour l'Europe du Nord, in Paris, equally owned by the State Bank of the USSR and the Bank for Foreign Trade in Moscow, gave the market its quite misleading Euro name, because the telegraphic address of this particular institution is Eurobank. Together with its sister institution in London, the Moscow Narodny, it was one of the earliest operators in this market.

But this alleged Marxist origin is carrying these early signs of Eurodollar practices too far. What they did was to begin to feed a free, open market in non-resident dollars and to reveal that it was a market in which wholesale dealers could operate at a 'reasonable' profit within the wide margins set by the somewhat rigid structure of

US domestic interest rates. The lesson was quickly learned, and its potential profitability appreciated by bankers, notably in London. In this context honourable mention must be made of Sir George Bolton, then recently liberated from the Bank of England and on the rampage as a commercial banker at the head of the Bank of London and South America.

Decline of sterling and rise of London as Eurocurrency centre

The speed with which London responded to this opportunity was in part due to the decline in the importance of sterling as an international commercial currency. This decline had been proceeding steadily since the end of the war; but, in order to defend it against speculation, fed by sterling credits to non-residents, it was ordained, in October 1968, that sterling acceptance credits and loans must not be made available to finance third-party transactions. Out went the bill on London as a prime instrument for the finance of international trade other than that in which the UK was directly involved.

London bankers are nothing if not adaptable. They quickly adjusted themselves to the use of other currencies, principally dollars, to fill the void created by sterling exchange control restrictions. Restrictions on the movement of funds out of the United States drove foreign dollar business out of the country, and exchange control affecting non-resident sterling credits provided an open-arm welcome for this expatriate dollar business in London.

Invasion of the City

This short history explains the advent of the market, London's role in its development, and, in consequence, the invasion of the City by branches, agencies and affiliates of foreign banks, not least American banks. It should be added that, though London provided some of the pioneers, the merchant adventurers in this quest for new business, it also provided horrified warnings by some of the most eminent members of the banking establishment, that these new-fangled markets were an artificial excrescence on the system of international finance and that they were likely to come to an early and, for the unwary, a painful end.

Some of the factors responsible for the emergence and growth of the Euro-currency markets have admittedly disappeared. The so-called *détente* between the US and the USSR should have removed the element of fear which kept Russian dollar balances away from domestic US banks. Moreover, the restrictions on the movement of funds out of the United States disappeared in January 1974, when the Foreign Credit Restraint Programme, the Foreign Direct Investment Programme and the Interest Equalisation Tax were abolished. In addition, the restraints through Regulation Q on the flexibility of interest rates on wholesale money had been removed from June 1970.

This relaxation of controls should have caused some of the Eurodollar business to drift back to the New York markets. In the event, some of the operations of American multi-national companies, which before 1974 would have been channelled through the Eurodollar markets, are now handled by the American banks as part and parcel of their normal domestic business. Yet the Eurodollar market has continued to grow—from $136 billion (the dollar element in the Eurocurrency money markets) at the end of 1973 to $275 billion in mid-1978.

Over these four and a half years, the total Eurocurrency money market grew from $200 billion to $400 billion. Any relative loss in the dollar element was made good by other currencies, notably by German marks and Swiss francs—and these parts of the Eurocurrency market have been stimulated by the restrictions placed by these countries on the unwanted *inflow* of funds. Here are further examples of the mixed parentage of these markets, the combination of restrictions at home and freedom in the context of the external, international markets.

3. TIME AND GEOGRAPHY: GROWTH OF LONDON EURODOLLAR MARKET

A larger share of the Eurodollar market has *not* moved to New York in part because of the clock. Most of the major money and capital markets of the world are having a late dinner, or are asleep, when New York is open for business. In this context London is far better placed on the parallels of longitude. There is an even more powerful reason for the weakness of the New York magnet in the kind of business transacted in the Eurocurrency markets. The nexus of US regulations prevents nationwide banking and deprives the New York market of the direct representation of banks registered outside the

State of New York. Many more American major banks are represented in London than in New York. And so we have seen the extraordinary paradox of Eurodollar loans for which the so-called 'tombstone' of participants[2] was made up almost exclusively of American banking names but for which the business was arranged through and in London.

It might be argued that if there is an economic miracle to be discerned in Britain's recent performance it is in the City of London's ability to remain a strong international financial centre, the strongest Eurocurrency market of them all, in spite of the handicaps of an unstable domestic currency, a somewhat unfavourable political climate, and fiscal deterrents to the inflow of foreign bankers. Part of this miracle has been handed to us on a plate by other centres and particularly by New York; but miracle it remains, none the less.

Quite apart from location and from the influences that may have affected its composition, it is quite evident that the Eurocurrency markets have acquired a magnitude and momentum which make them an essential, enduring and, in so far as we may use that adjective, a permanent part of the mechanism of international finance.

Cause of expansion: credit creation or balance of payments?

What are the forces and processes that have contributed to this giant's phenomenal growth? The theory has been advanced by eminent economists[3] that the Eurocurrency float, or pool, is simply the product of the commercial banks' mystic power to create credit —not, it is true, out of nothing, but out of a comparatively small reserve base of liquid assets.

I entirely reject this explanation. I cannot believe that a chain of Eurobanks can create, shall we say, dollars independently of the wishes or policies of the Federal Reserve authorities. It is out of the question that, for example, a French and a German bank can by their bilateral, or multilateral, operations create sterling outside the volition of the Bank of England. If this power existed, and since there is no ultimate controller and lender of last resort in the Eurocurrency market, we can be sure it would have been used, perhaps

---

[2] The banks participating in the issue and whose names are printed in the prospectus.

[3] Among them Professor Milton Friedman, in 'The Euro-dollar Market: Some First Principles', *Morgan Guaranty Survey*, October 1969.

abused, on a much larger scale. If this magic power existed, why this self-denying ordinance not to use it to the full?

The currencies in this non-resident Euro-circulation are, and must be, part and parcel of the balances of payments of the countries whose currencies are thus held in banks outside their frontiers. The Euro-dollar float is part of the complex nexus of transactions that have gone to make up the US balance of payments—viewed in its widest liquidity definition and not on an official transactions basis.

Lagoons and pools

Yet it is perhaps possible to reconcile these two schools of thought: the credit-creation and the balance-of-payments explanations of the Eurocurrency markets. The largest of them, the Eurodollar market in non-resident dollars, is and has been linked to the domestic dollar market through side doors, some of them clandestine in the days of rigorous control of capital outflows from the United States, but since January 1974 through a wide-open front door. US banks can and do shift funds to and from the Eurodollar market in response to interest-rate differentials and availability of funds. It is therefore quite inappropriate and misleading to refer to a Eurodollar 'pool' as though it were self-enclosed. It is not a 'pool'; it is a *lagoon* linked to the ocean of money and credit supply in the United States. Dollars flow in from the domestic ocean to the Euro-lagoon or *vice-versa* as a result of transactions that are part of the US balance of payments. Since the magic of credit creation certainly operates within the United States, under the eagle eye and control of the Federal Reserve authorities, and since there is freedom of movement between domestic and Eurodollars, it follows that the magic of credit creation *affects* the Eurodollar market, but does not operate *within* it.

All the illustrations of this alleged operation of the magic within the market[4] are based on a most glaring technical fallacy. They assume that a commercial bank maintains a liquidity reserve of, say, 10 per cent against Eurocurrency liabilities. This may be the Euro-banking world as it appears to an outsider; but it is not the real world of Eurobanking. In Britain foreign currency deposits become liable to reserve requirements only insofar as there is a net foreign currency

---

[4] Fritz Machlup, 'Eurodollar Creation: A Mystery Story', *Banca Natzionale del Lavoro Quarterly Review*, September 1970, pp. 219-260, reprinted Princeton, December 1970.

liability. As banks normally maintain a virtual balance between their Euro liabilities and assets, the reserve requirements play at most a minimal role. When a bank borrows Eurodollars, it on lends them *in toto,* with the purpose of profit. If it maintained a 10 per cent cash or liquidity reserve against this liability, it would soon be out of the Eurocurrency business. The narrow margins do not allow the luxury of cash reserves.

4. INTERNATIONAL MARKETS AND INTERNATIONAL FINANCING

What has been the significance of these markets for international finance—both in the commercial banking and central banking contexts? They have emphasised and confirmed the preponderance of the US dollar as an international transactions and reserve currency. The dollar has throughout been the preponderant element in the Euro-markets. The relative importance of other currencies has recently been increasing, notably that of the West German mark and the Swiss franc. But they have grown in the role of investment and 'funk money' currencies, not as commercial vehicle currencies. The dollar remains supreme. The figures speak for themselves: at the latest count it represented 73 per cent of the Eurocurrency market, and 65 per cent of the Eurobonds outstanding had been issued in dollar terms.

The other currencies so far in Eurobond issues have been Deutsch-marks, guilders and Canadian dollars. Towards the end of 1977 the Bank of England gave permission for a number of Eurosterling bond issues, some for UK companies with overseas interests, others for EEC-related institutions. London has failed to secure its full share of the secondary market in Eurobonds. This is because of the deter-rent effect of exchange control, particularly the impact of the invest-ment premium and, until January 1978, of the surrender rule.[5] These self-inflicted wounds have had wider effect since they have virtually banished investment and arbitrage business in overseas and all 'premium-worthy' securities.

---

[5] The 25 per cent surrender rule prevented the development of an active second-ary Eurobond market in London. This and other defects of exchange control are discussed in Robert Miller and John B. Wood, *Exchange Control for Ever?*, Research Monograph 33, IEA, 1979.

The supremacy of the dollar: reserve currency role reinforced

This confirmation by the Eurocurrency markets of the supremacy of the dollar as the currency used in international trade and finance has been accompanied by its retention of the role of reserve currency. In this context it goes from strength to strength. The Finance Ministers and their deputies and experts may decide that the age of reserve currencies is past, that their role is being phased out; but events cock an independent snook at them. Since the end of 1971, when the dismissal of the by then unconvertible dollar was to begin, the international reserves kept in the form of US dollars have increased from $50 billion to $146 billion. Over the same period total reserves maintained in the form of currencies other than that of the holder have risen from $75 billion to $203 billion. The experts propose, the reality of practical life disposes.

What should be emphasised is, first, the big uplift the Eurocurrency markets have given to the dollar as a commercial and reserve currency, and, secondly, the magnificent way in which those markets have responded to the searching, searing test of the oil crisis. The disturbance to international balances of payments caused by the arbitrary quintupling of the price of oil would have been immeasurably more damaging to exchange stability and to the world economy had it not been for the way in which the smooth-functioning Eurocurrency markets—mostly dollars—tackled the task of recycling the surpluses of the OPEC countries. They handled $25 billion of the OPEC surplus of $56 billion in 1974, an estimated $15 billion of the reduced surplus of around $32 billion in 1975, and $16 billion out of the surplus of $36 billion in 1976. Had it not been for the Eurocurrency markets the burden on the inter-central bank swap systems[6] would have been many times that which had to be sustained in these years. The bulk of that Eurocurrency recycling was done through the London market.

No national capital market could have handled the investment of the enormous surpluses accruing to the oil exporting countries or the finance of the equally large deficits of the oil importers. One can claim for the Eurocurrency markets that by their contribution to the recycling process they averted a much deeper oil-induced recession

---

[6] If central bank intervention had been called upon to play a greater role in the recycling of OPEC surpluses the consequent disturbances of money supplies and price stability would have been even greater than they were.

than that which has had to be endured. They have also averted what could have been a major drift into protectionism.

It might be argued, on the other hand, that the very smoothness and efficiency of the market provided an unduly easy entry for some borrowers. That should bring its own corrective remedy, as has already become evident in the difficulties being met by some less-developed countries in meeting their Eurocurrency loan and bond obligations and in the mark-up of rates quoted in the market above the basic London Inter-Bank rate.

Destructive or constructive?

It cannot be denied that the expansion of this market and the freedom of operation which is its life blood have created a monster that could be destructive as well as benign and constructive. This mass of liquidity, much of it borrowed at very short term, is a sword of Damocles hanging over the world's foreign exchange markets. Now that floating rates of exchange are legalised and regarded as the 'norm', it presents a formidable challenge to the major monetary authorities of the world, a call to strengthen their collaboration, their mutual and collective defences.

But there is re-assurance to be drawn even from this common danger. Its recognition must strengthen the forces making for harmonisation of domestic monetary policies. For some time the Commission of the European Economic Community has been studying the problem of integrating and uniting the forces of the capital markets in its member countries. A study in depth, the Segré Report,[7] has analysed the problem and made proposals. But what may seem a difficult, intractable project is solving itself by the growth and spread of the Eurocurrency markets in which all member countries operate and to which they all contribute. This shows that the adaptability and dynamism of market forces if left to themselves and given freedom to operate will accomplish far more—and far more effectively—than the *dirigiste* plans of experts and of bureaucracy, however competent.

The growth of the market has created problems for the participating banks. Their capital resources have not always been able to keep pace with the growth in deposit liabilities that accompanied

---

[7] *Development of a European Capital Market*, Report of a group of experts chaired by M. Segré, published by the EEC Commission, Brussels, 1966.

their role as intermediaries in this massive movement of funds. This deficiency could be one of the explanations for the strange, mysterious appearance of certain otherwise unexceptionable American banks on the so-called 'problem list'[8] published by the Federal Reserve authorities. The situation certainly calls for the strictest supervision and control—as indeed it is receiving from the banking authorities in the countries mainly concerned.

A warning to London

The participation of London institutions in this market requires a word of warning as well as one of commendation. London banks were prominent in the pioneering stages of the market. The BIS figures show that on 30 June, 1978, London-based banks held external 'Euro' deposits equivalent to $169,400 million out of a total of $400,000 million for the eight reporting European countries. An even higher proportion of the business in Eurocurrencies is done in the City of London than that indicated by these deposit figures.

Later figures published in the Bank of England *Quarterly Bulletin* show that the total foreign currency deposits of banks in the UK (including the branches of foreign banks) exceeded their sterling deposits, namely £140·1 billion as against £63·9 billion. Apart from those applying to foreign banks, the foreign currency deposits of domestic sterling-based banks amounted to the equivalent of £26·7 billion as against sterling deposits of £51·6 billion.

For banks capitalised in sterling this huge participation in foreign currency business has created problems of somewhat overstretched ratios of capital to total deposit liabilities. Given the expansion of foreign currency deposits and the depreciation in the exchange value of sterling, the 'solvency ratio' has suffered and has had to be defended by a reinforcement of the sterling banks' own resources by new issues of shares and in some cases by borrowing in foreign currencies.

This reservation is a technical one and detracts in no way from the highly commendable manner in which London banks have from its earliest days secured the lion's share of this vast and still expanding Eurocurrency market.

---

[8] These are lists of banks to which the Federal Reserve authorities draw cautionary attention when foreign defaults occur.

Eurocurrency business lost to tax havens

A more important reservation concerns the future. During the past three years the external deposits of offshore banking centres in the Caribbean (mainly the Bahamas and Cayman Islands) and the Far East (Hong Kong and Singapore) have almost trebled—a rate of expansion far exceeding that in the UK. Some of the offshore banking centres have few banks but an abundance of name-plates for agencies and representatives. They share, above all, extremely generous and lenient fiscal advantages. They are the tax havens to which an increasing volume of Eurocurrency business is transmitted after being processed in London and other genuine banking centres.

The lesson is self-evident: high costs, high rents and rates, high personal and corporate taxation could propel more of this business —not only in its book-keeping aspects, but finally in the processing stages—to these tax havens. An offshore banking centre needs skilled dealers and a first-class communications system. It will attract business if the conventional, traditional financial centres repel it by excessive taxation and by engendering fears of bank nationalisation or other forms of State intervention.

City of London market resilience

The international money and capital markets are here to stay. They are a proof of the creative dynamism of private enterprise and its ability to escape from the restrictions imposed on the freedom of domestic markets. The City of London's participation in the international market has been preponderant and lucrative. The traditions and experience of London as a great financial centre, and the history of sterling as a major international currency, have served it well. London banks have shown once again a capacity for adaptation and adjustment which no other comparable centre has so far matched. Above all, the informality, self-discipline and ease of entry for foreign banks have given London a diversity and catholicity of representation which are also unique. But the market in which these qualities have flourished is highly competitive, constantly testing the ingenuity of the participating countries and institutions. London's pre-eminence in this market is not to be taken for granted. It needs constant defence against competition from without and some enemies from within.

5. CONCLUSION

The misnamed Eurocurrency markets are here to stay, provided they are not interfered with by well-meaning or other interventionists and controllers. They will grow as restrictions continue to hamper the freedom of operation of domestic money and capital markets—and provided we maintain non-resident convertibility of the major currencies and freedom in the flow of funds from the domestic to these non-resident external markets.

Achievements of Eurocurrency markets

These markets have become an essential part of the international financial mechanism. They have been an invaluable clearing house, receiving the surpluses and financing the deficits of countries affected in one direction or the other by the oil crisis. In this way they have eased the burden which would otherwise have fallen on national monetary authorities and on the IMF.

The Eurocurrency market, moreover, has acquired the substance and flexibility which enables it to cope with capital projects, such as off-shore oil exploration and development, which would outstrip the resources and potential of the national domestic money and capital markets.

Not the least achievement of the Eurocurrency market has been its ability to reprocess a large part of the credit passing through it. On balance the borrowers of Eurocurrencies have required longer-term credit than the primary suppliers have been prepared to grant. The intermediaries, therefore, have on the whole been called upon to borrow short and to lend somewhat longer. The adoption of the roll-over technique[9] for the Eurocurrency market and perhaps the floating-rate bond for the Eurobond market has met part of the problem, namely, the risk of riding the ever-changing interest-rate curve when the length of maturities on each side of the balance sheet are not matched.

But there are other risks. The non-availability of currencies when the roll-over has to be undertaken, for example, has in some cases been covered—at a cost, of course—by negotiating stand-by credits with banks in the country of the currency concerned—in Eurodollar

---

[9] The rate of interest on a medium-term loan is adjusted to prevailing market rates every three, six or 12 months and the loan is renewed or 'rolled over' for that period.

business with American banks. These are examples of the ingenuity and inventiveness that are of the essence of the Eurocurrency markets.

Passing the test

These markets have withstood the test of the recession and of the difficulties experienced in the world of banking—the fringe bank collapses, the losses incurred in the foreign exchange markets—which have already called into being measures of control, supervision and regulation, including the allocation of ultimate responsibility for the commitments of foreign subsidiaries and consortium banks.

Provided this healthy and desirable supervision does not overreach itself into the realms of restrictive exchange controls, I foresee continued expansion of both Eurocurrency and Eurobond markets. The world economy demands their flexibility and capacity for improvisation, for meeting the ever-changing needs of a capital-hungry world.